You give them something to eat

You give them something to eat

MINISTERING
when you think you can't

Joe Paprocki

AVE MARIA PRESS   Notre Dame, Indiana 46556

© 1998 by Ave Maria Press, Inc.

All rights reserved. No part of this book may be used or reproduced in any manner whatsoever without written permission, except for materials appearing on pages labeled, "resource" and except in the case of reprints used in the context of reviews.

International Standard Book Number: 0-87793-655-2

Cover design by: Kathy Coleman

Text design by Brian C. Conley

Printed and bound in the United States of America.

Library of Congress Cataloging-in-Publication Data

Paprocki, Joe.

You give them something to eat : ministering when you think you can't / Joe Paprocki.

     p.   cm.

Includes bibliographical references.

ISBN 0-87793-655-2

1. Church work—Catholic Church. 2. Lay ministry—Catholic Church. 3. Pastoral theology—Catholic Church. 4. Catholic Church—Membership. I. Title.

BX2347.P27   1998

253—dc21

                           98-19807

                           CIP

To my parents, John and Veronica, who led me to the Table where all hunger is satisfied. And to Fr. Jack Daley who taught me how to set the Table and now serves as *maitre d'* at the Great Banquet.

I would like to thank Mike Amodei for thinking that I could provide people with something to "eat" in the way of a book; Fr. Eugene LaVerdiere, SSS, for teaching me about the Bread of Life; my friends and colleagues at the Office for Religious Education in the Archdiocese of Chicago for their support and encouragement; and my wife, Joanne, and our children, Mike and Amy, for their steadfast love.

Contents

Introduction

"My pastor asked me to coordinate the RCIA process next year. Why me? I'm no theologian. What am I supposed to teach these people? I don't know where to begin."

"How do I get myself into these things? Sure I've been a catechist for five years. But DRE? Taking care of my own class was challenging enough . . . the thought of coordinating the whole program is overwhelming!"

"At a parish town hall meeting, I made the mistake of speaking up about how our church needs to do more for our youth. You guessed it . . . they asked me to head up youth ministry. Sure I recognized a need. But how am I supposed to come up with some way to get them more involved in church? Me and my big mouth!"

"I've been a Minister of Care for a couple of years already. I consider it a privilege to bring communion to the sick, but they need so much more and I just wonder sometimes if I'm giving them what they really need."

Sound familiar? Few of us in pastoral ministry have been spared such moments of self-doubt. Even if we've been involved in ministry for a number of years, the thought of taking on a new project for our church or tending to the needs of a large group of people in the parish can seem overwhelming, prompting us to ask, "How can I possibly satisfy the many 'hungers' and needs of so many people with what little I have?"

If you've ever experienced this kind of self-doubt, you're in good company. The first disciples themselves felt very much the same way many times during their tenure with Jesus. Often they wondered about Jesus' true identity. Sometimes they questioned why they followed. One scripture story, however, captures their experience like a photograph and provides revealing insight to us as to how to cope with the seemingly overwhelming needs of those we serve. The story is the Feeding of the 5000.

Surrounded by an audience of 5000 hungry people, the disciples engage in a fascinating exchange with Jesus that results in the ultimate transformation of a hopeless and desperate situation into a lavish banquet with a menu so large that everyone has enough left over to take home. I imagine that the disciples felt more than slightly overwhelmed when they looked out at the hungry crowd of 5000 and heard Jesus utter the words, "Give them something to eat!" No doubt at least one of the twelve responded by saying, "Jesus, you've got to be kidding!" Like us, the disciples felt ill-equipped to carry out such an enormous task. Yet, Jesus had confidence in his disciples, and he has confidence in US!

As we survey the hungry crowds in our own ministerial settings and doubt our ability to feed them properly, Jesus says to us, "YOU . . . give them something to eat!" We may feel that our own talents and skills make the five loaves and two fish look like a smorgasbord. Yet, Jesus is counting on us to feed his people. While our ministry may sometimes feel overwhelming, the story of the Feeding of the 5000 can teach us to "set the table" so that the miraculous power of Jesus can provide those we serve with the nourishment they need . . . and still have something left over!

> When he disembarked and saw the vast crowd, his heart was moved with pity for them, for they were like sheep without a shepherd; and he began to teach them many things. By now it was already late and his disciples approached him and said, "This is a deserted place and it is already very late. Dismiss them so that they can go to the surrounding farms and villages and buy themselves something to eat." He said to them in reply, "Give them some food yourselves." But they said to him, "Are we to buy two hundred days' wages worth of food and give it to them to eat?" He asked them, "How many loaves do you have? Go and see." And when they had found out they said, "Five loaves and two fish." So he gave orders to have them sit down in groups on the green grass. The people took their places in rows by hundreds and by fifties. Then, taking the five loaves and the two fish and looking up to heaven, he said the blessing, broke the loaves, and gave them to his disciples to set before the people; he also divided the two fish among them all. They all ate and were satisfied. And they picked up twelve wicker baskets full of fragments and what was left of the fish. Those who ate of the loaves were five thousand men.

> —Mark 6:34-44

CHAPTER ONE

Send Them Away!

The Reluctant Minister

Reluctant Ministers

There is a long and noble tradition of reluctance running through the pages of salvation history. Moses responded to the burning bush by saying, "Who am I that I should go to Pharaoh?" Jeremiah answered the call to prophecy with the response of, "Ah, Lord, I know not how to speak; I am too young!" Jonah's reluctance and anxiety ran so high that he boarded a ship and set sail in the opposite direction of Nineveh. Mary asked her angelic messenger, "How can this be since I do not know man?" Jesus himself said, "Father, if it is your will, take this cup away from me." In more recent times, Dr. Martin Luther King Jr. admitted that when he was asked to take the reins of the struggle for civil rights, he hesitated because he was just beginning to enjoy the fruits of his ministry as pastor of a small congregation named the Ebeneezer Baptist Church and preferred to stay out of the limelight.

The first disciples, then, find themselves in good company. In the tradition of Moses and the prophets right on down to Dr. Martin Luther King Jr., the disciples responded to the challenge to serve the needs of others with reluctance. When the disciples realized that the day was growing long, the crowd was growing larger, and appetites were rapidly expanding, their initial reaction was the classic: "SEND THEM AWAY! Let someone else take care of these people! Let them take care of themselves!"

To be reluctant means to have some doubts about your own capabilities. This is not necessarily a bad thing. A few ounces of self-doubt can separate us from recklessness on the one hand and arrogance on the other. Reluctance to handle something on our own often drives us to seek partnership with others and avoids the temptation to operate as a lone ranger or superhero. In church ministry, there is no place for lone rangers or superheroes! Nevertheless, we are not to let some self-doubt about our own capabilities cripple us to the point where we refuse to take on a particular ministerial challenge. Our reluctance doesn't excuse us from accepting a challenge, as difficult as it might seem.

For Reflection

- What ministry or part of my ministry am I experiencing feelings of reluctance toward and why?
- Whose needs seem so overwhelming that my temptation is to say, "Send them away"?

No One in Their Right Mind

The disciples had a pretty good argument in their favor:
- the crowd was vast
- it was getting late
- they were in a deserted place
- it would cost 200 days' wages to feed such a crowd— money they did not have
- all they had were five loaves and two fish!

With precise logic, they presented these facts to Jesus as though saying, "*Now* will you send them away? You can't really expect us to take on such an overwhelming task!" The disciples were right. Logic dictates that it would be best to send them away. Unfortunately for the disciples (and fortunately for the 5000), the disciples were *not* conversing with the famous logic-driven science officer from Star Trek, Mr. Spock, who no doubt would have agreed. Jesus defies logic and employs *imagination*. Sure, Jesus sees the problem just as clearly as the disciples, but he also sees beyond the reality to the possibilities and potential of the situation. Jesus, like all people of vision, is not out of touch with reality, but has the gift of seeing beyond the limits of reality to a *preferred* reality.

In our own ministry, we may have some very good arguments about why it defies logic to take on a certain project or challenge:

"I work full time . . . when will I be able to get this project done?"

"I need more time to myself."

"I don't have the theological background that Father has. What can I offer?"

"Our parish doesn't have the money it takes to accomplish this project properly."

"People are too busy these days to be bothered with church activities."

And so on.

There is no reasoning with these and other arguments we may come up with. They are sound and logical. Yet, Jesus, who sees what we see, challenges us to see beyond the logical limitations. He challenges us to use our imaginations to explore the possibilities and potential that exist *despite* the logical limitations. When you get down to it, the very notion of living as a Christian is not logical. Jesus says to us, "When you were baptized, you accepted the challenge to follow me to the cross . . . perhaps the most illogical decision you've ever made. Don't get logical on me now!"

For Reflection

- What are some very logical reasons I should *not* get involved in a certain ministry or aspect of a certain ministry?
- Beyond logic, what are the possibilities and potential that exist in accepting a role in this ministry or aspect of ministry?

Lord, I Am Not Worthy

Several years ago, I asked a long-time parishioner to consider becoming a eucharistic minister. She had been a pillar in the parish for over twenty-five years. She was married there; her children had gone through the religious education programs. She was involved in the Women's Club, scripture study, and a variety of other parish activities. Her response to my invitation was less than enthusiastic. Upon pursuing the topic with her, she said, "I don't know if I am worthy to minister the eucharist." I was both amazed and impressed that a person with such outstanding credentials would respond in such a way. Amazed because of the respect I knew she had in the parish. Impressed because she had the humility to doubt herself.

Her reaction was not unlike that of the Roman centurion who begged Jesus to cure his son. As Jesus got up to go perform the miracle, the centurion interrupted: "Lord, I am not worthy to have you enter my home." In this moment of self-doubt, we come to the realization that, on our own, we are incapable of doing what we have been asked to do. Jesus, however, does not let us wallow there within the realm of self-pity but instead challenges us to transform these feelings of self-doubt into a healthy humility and admission of our dependence upon a higher power, our heavenly Father.

But Only Say the Word

Though Moses, Jeremiah, and Jonah all felt reluctant, they did carry out what the Lord had called them to do. Mary responded initially with incredulity but eventually said, "I am the servant of the Lord . . . let it be done to me as you say." Jesus quickly moved past his hesitation in the garden of Gethsemane and said, "Yet, not my will, but yours be done." The centurion did not feel worthy, but he *did* ask Jesus to perform the miracle: "Lord, I am not worthy to have you enter my house, *but only say the word and my servant shall be healed!*"

Our feelings of self-doubt and reluctance should not stand in the way of the power of God. The disciples gave it their best shot at convincing Jesus of the hopelessness of the situation. Jesus listened, nodded his head, and proceeded to give the word that resulted in a miracle meal. The disciples did not let their feelings of self-doubt, unworthiness, or reluctance stand in the way of letting the power of God's word work through them.

We may have a million and one reasons *not* to take on the ministry that we are being called to. At least a million of those reasons are most likely sound and logical. Yet, Jesus calls us to defy logic . . . to overcome reluctance and self-doubt . . . and to use our newly found humility to say, "Lord, I may not feel worthy, but only say the word, and your people *will* be fed!"

For Reflection

- In what area of my ministry do I need to say, "Your will be done," or, "Let it be done to me as you say"?
- Who are some people I know of who defy logic in order to serve God's people?
- What is a small step I can take today to overcome my reluctance, turn my self-doubt into a healthy humility, and serve God's people despite the million and one reasons I can think of not to?

Scripture for Prayer

What will separate us from the love of Christ? Will anguish, or distress, or persecution, or famine, or nakedness, or peril, or the sword? As it is written: "For your sake we are being slain all the day; we are looked upon as sheep to be slaughtered."
No, in all these things we conquer overwhelmingly through him who loved us. For I am convinced that neither death, nor life, nor angels, nor principalities, nor present things, nor future things, nor powers, nor height, nor depth, nor any other creature will be able to separate us from the love of God in Christ Jesus our Lord.

—Romans 8:35-39

Say not, "I am too young." To whomever I send you, you shall go; whatever I command you, you shall speak. Have no fear before them, because I am with you to deliver you, says the Lord.
Then the Lord extended his hand and touched my mouth, saying,
See, I place my words in your mouth! This day I set you over nations and over kingdoms.

—Jeremiah 1:7-10

Three times I begged the Lord about this, that it might leave me, but he said to me, "My grace is sufficient for you, for power is made perfect in weakness." I will rather boast most gladly of my weaknesses, in order that the power of Christ may dwell with me. Therefore, I am content with weaknesses, insults, hardships, persecutions, and constraints, for the sake of Christ; for when I am weak, then I am strong.

—2 Corinthians 12:8-10

In Their Own Words

One day, after finishing school, I was called to a little church down in Montgomery, Alabama. And I started preaching there . . . things were going well . . . it was a marvelous experience. But one day, a year later, a lady by the name of Rosa Parks decided that she wasn't gonna take it any longer . . . she stayed in her bus seat. It was the beginning of a movement. The people of Montgomery asked me to serve as a spokesman and to . . . lead the boycott. I couldn't say no. Things were going well for the first few days but then . . . it came to the point that some days more than forty telephone calls came in threatening my life, the life of my family, the life of my children. I was frustrated and bewildered. It got to the point where I couldn't take it any longer . . . I was weak. Something said to me, "You can't call on daddy anymore . . . you can't even call on momma now. You gotta call on that something; on that person that your daddy used to tell you about . . . that power that can make a way out of no way." I prayed a prayer out loud, "Lord, I'm down here trying to do what's right. But Lord, I must confess that I'm weak now . . . I'm faltering . . . I'm losing my courage." It seemed to me that I could hear an inner voice saying to me, "Martin Luther . . . Stand up for righteousness! Stand up for justice! Stand up for truth! And lo, I will be with you even until the end of the world." Yes, sometimes I feel discouraged and feel my work's in vain, but then, the Holy Spirit revives my soul again: "There *is* a balm in Gilead to make the wounded whole. There *is* a balm in Gilead to heal the sin-sick soul!"

—Dr. Martin Luther King, Jr.

Do the Right Thing!

I once took a group of high school students to visit Fr. Larry Craig, a Chicago priest involved in prison ministry. One of the students asked him, "How many lives have you turned around?" Fr. Craig thought about it for a second and replied, "Let's see. I've been doing this for about fifteen years. That's about 5000 'juvies' . . . I'd say about *six*. Next question?" I had to interrupt. "Excuse me Father, in 15 years and over 5000 inmates, you can recall turning around only about six lives? Why do you do it? *How* do you do it? What keeps you motivated?" Fr. Larry replied, "I do it because it's the right thing to do. Jesus said, 'When I was in prison you visited me.' He didn't say 'When I was a teenager, you took me on a ski trip.' Next question?" I was amazed at this man's sense of commitment and his ability to defy logic. He looked at a crowd of 5000 and instead of saying "Send them away!" he started distributing whatever loaves and fish he could find.

21

In our ministries, we face our own crowds of 5000. The logical thing would be to send them away. But what would be the *right* thing to do?

Reluctance Checklist

On a scale of 1-10 (1 being *extremely reluctant*; 10 being *extremely willing*), identify how you feel about:

____ Volunteering at work for a project that involves little or no extra compensation

____ Collaborating in ministry with someone you don't get along with

____ Taking time to listen to a friend when you're busy

____ Participating in an ongoing ministry at your parish

____ Volunteering for a community service project

____ Serving as a chaperone at a teenagers' dance

____ Taking on a new project or ministry

____ Chairing a committee for a special event

____ Serving in a capacity for which you have no training

____ Spending time with someone who is lonely

Suggested Activities

- Read about a person well known for doing ministry in the service of others (e.g., Mother Teresa of Calcutta, Harriet Tubman, Dr. Martin Luther King Jr., Bishop Oscar Romero, or Dorothy Day). How did this person overcome feelings of reluctance and self-doubt and participate in a ministry that defied logic?

- Brainstorm a list of people who have served you or your parish selflessly. Reflect on how easy it would have been for them *not* to do the service they did, and what leads them to do what they do.
- Create your own "mini-Lent" over the next forty hours. Draw up a list of a few disciplines you can practice to strengthen your resolve to overcome reluctance in your ministry.
- Start small . . . do one thing today that you did not plan to do and that you have every reason not to do. Do it because it's the right thing to do!

A Prayer in Times of Reluctance

Jesus, I feel as though I'm being asked to feed thousands of people with a few morsels of food. I don't feel capable. I'm not sure I even want to do this. Give me the strength and courage I need to make the right decision and to do what is best for those I serve. Open my eyes to see with imagination. Grant me the trust I need to believe that you "can make a way out of no way." Teach me how to set the table so that your food may give life to those I serve. Transform my reluctance and self-doubt into humility, that I may give of myself humbly and selflessly. Place the basket in my hands and send me on my way knowing that your love and grace will multiply as I give of myself to others.

CHAPTER TWO

YOU Give Them Something to Eat!

Assuming Responsibility

Are You Talking to Me?

When Jesus said words to the effect of, "*You* give them something to eat," I'm certain that the disciples looked around expecting to see that a catering caravan had just pulled up behind them. Imagine how the disciples must have felt when they realized Jesus was speaking to *them*! Probably a lot like you felt when you were asked to take up the ministry that awaits you! The famous tough guy line from the movie *Taxi Driver* sums up the common reaction:

"Are you talking to *me*?"

The disciples had already witnessed Jesus perform some pretty impressive miracles. They enjoyed standing by passively and watching Jesus restore sight to the blind, heal the lame, and open the ears of the deaf. They had no problem acting as bystanders and cheering while Jesus displayed his mighty power much the same way many of the

Chicago Bulls used to enjoy standing around while Michael Jordan scored another fifty or sixty points. As long as the disciples were wearing the right jersey and cheering for the right guy, everything was fine. But this time, Jesus was looking to his disciples to get involved in the game plan. Jesus put together three little letters that struck fear into the disciples' hearts: Y-O-U!

At some point, someone put those three little letters together and tossed them in your direction in connection with a certain ministry that is now your responsibility. YOU can take on the RCIA. YOU can serve on the Parish Council. YOU can be the new youth minister. YOU can bring the eucharist to the sick. YOU can coordinate religious education. YOU can teach the pre-schoolers. YOU, YOU, YOU. It's as if the greatest basketball player who ever played passed up the winning shot, passed you the ball instead, and said, "Here, you do it."

"Are you talking to *me?*"

Yes, Jesus is talking to you. Jesus is calling YOU to take on some responsibility for feeding God's people. Jesus is asking YOU to set the table for a feast he is about to serve. Jesus is not about to let you stand on the sideline when there's a game on the line. He's chosen you for his team and he's put you in the starting lineup. It's time to get to work!

For Reflection

- What was your first reaction to being asked to take on a new ministry? What qualities do you possess that may have led to your being asked?

- Who is someone in ministry that you have been watching "from the sidelines," and how can you hope to emulate him or her?

Don't Just Stand There

The artwork in a children's picture Bible you grew up with may have portrayed the scene of Jesus feeding the 5000 in this manner: Jesus raises his hands to heaven while his disciples stand idly by with looks of wonder and awe on their faces as tons of bread and fish miraculously appear. Unfortunately, those pictures do not accurately reflect what really happened. If anything, scripture tells us that the complete opposite of this portrayal is true: the *disciples* do most of the work while Jesus remains in the background. Jesus provides the power, but the disciples are the ones who work up a sweat doing the following:

- taking inventory of resources
- convincing 5000 people to be seated
- convincing 5000 people to break up into small groups
- distributing the bread
- distributing the fish
- gathering up all the leftovers

Yes, Jesus provided the power, but the disciples were the ones who raised their sails, so to speak, to catch the driving force of the Spirit and set sail into miracle land. Perhaps it is from this story that the famous saying, "God helps those who help themselves," came about, for if you look closely at the scripture passage, nowhere does it say that Jesus multiplied the loaves and fish! All it says is that he raised his eyes to heaven, said a blessing, and directed the disciples to begin distribution. The miracle occurs when somehow, through the efforts of twelve organizers, 5000 people find enough to go around.

All of this was made possible because twelve people chose not to stand around but instead got involved.

It's like the story of the person who prays to God night after night after night to win the lottery but to no avail. Finally, God responds: "It would help if you bought a ticket!"

We need to conspire, so to speak, with the power of God. We may be reluctant. We may be surprised. We may feel inadequate. But if we tap into the power of the One who provides life-giving bread, we, too, will be able to satisfy some pretty hearty spiritual appetites.

For Reflection

- How are you already feeding others in your ministerial setting?
- When was a time you tapped into the power of God and succeeded in nourishing others?
- Recall an experience from your own life when God helped you as you helped yourself.

Do You Believe in Miracles?

Many of us can recall that winter day in 1980 when the United States Olympic ice hockey team, on a goal from little-known captain Mike Eruzione, defeated the mighty Soviet Union team 3-2 for the gold medal. The Americans were not supposed to win. This team was a ragtag collection of amateurs going up against finely tuned and admirably conditioned soldiers who played hockey for a living. With the seconds counting down, the dream blossomed into reality. As time ran out, sportscaster Al Michaels shouted out, "Do you believe in miracles?" to which a nation responded with a resounding "Yes!"

How did this happen? Perhaps the story of how a group of young and inexperienced athletes teamed together, worked hard, dedicated themselves, and believed in themselves can serve to illustrate how miracles like the feeding of the 5000 can still occur today.

From time to time, people will ask, "How come miracles don't happen anymore? They happened in the Bible all the time. Why not today?" The 1980 Olympic ice hockey gold medal is just one example of how miracles still can and do occur today. Some are flashy. Others are fairly mundane. Yet, miracles do indeed occur when people say "yes" to the invitation to get involved. Miracles occur when people like you make a commitment to try.

Miracles happen in ministry when ordinary people stop standing around and get involved. I have seen children's interest and love for the Lord soar because of the creativity and dedication of a catechist. I have seen senior citizens who were paralyzed in fear and lethargy get up and walk the road of involvement and activity because of the compassion and energy of young adult volunteers. I have seen parish organizations that were lost and mired in confusion discover their way because of the vision and clarity of a dedicated parishioner who volunteered to lead them. You see, Jesus always provides the food as long as we volunteer to set the table. Miracles still do happen!

If not us,

WHO?

If not here,

WHERE?

If not now,

WHEN?

If not for the Kingdom,

WHY?

Dare the Dream.

(National Catholic Vocation Council Poster)

Scripture for Prayer

After this the Lord appointed seventy-two others whom he sent ahead of him in pairs to every town and place he intended to visit. He said to them, "The harvest is abundant but the laborers are few; so ask the master of the harvest to send out laborers for his harvest."

—Luke 10:1-2

I pray for them . . . so that they may share my joy completely. I gave them your word, and the world hated them, because they do not belong to the world any more than I belong to the world. I do not ask that you take them out of the world, but that you keep them from the evil one. They do not belong to the world any more than I belong to the world. Consecrate them in the truth. Your word is truth. As you sent me into the world, so I sent them into the world. And I consecrate myself for them, so that they also may be consecrated in truth.

—John 17:9, 13-19

Then David spoke to Saul: "Let your majesty not lose courage. I am at your service to go and fight this Philistine." But Saul answered David, "You cannot go up against this Philistine and fight with him, for you are only a youth; while he has been a warrior from his youth." David continued: "The Lord, who delivered me from the claws of the lion and the bear, will also keep me safe from

31

the clutches of this Philistine." Saul answered David, "Go! the Lord will be with you!"

—1 Samuel 17:32-33, 37

For Reflection

- What miracles are already occurring in your ministerial setting?
- What and where is Jesus sending you to "harvest"?
- What "Goliaths" do you face in your ministry? Who are the "Sauls" who seem to be telling you that you can't go up against the giant?

In Their Own Words

From the moment they are born, children depend on a host of other "grown-ups"—grandparents, neighbors, teachers, ministers, employers, political leaders, and untold others who touch their lives directly and indirectly. Each of us plays a part in every child's life: it takes a village to raise a child. I chose that old African proverb . . . because it offers a timeless reminder that children will thrive only if their families thrive and if the whole of society cares enough to provide for them. There's an old saying I love: You can't roll up your sleeves and get to work if you're still ringing your hands.

—Hillary Rodham Clinton, *It Takes a Village*
(Touchstone, 1996)

I don't know Who—or What—put the question. I don't know when it was put. I don't even remember answering. But at some moment, I did answer yes to Someone—or Something—and at that hour, I was certain existence is meaningful and that, therefore, my life in self-surrender had a goal.

—Dag Hammarskjöld, *The Oxford Book of Prayer*
(Oxford University Press, 1994)

Prayer in action is love and love in action is service. Try to give unconditionally whatever a person needs in the moment. The point is to do something however small and show you care through your actions by giving your time. We are all God's children, so it is important to share His gifts. Do not worry about why problems exist in the world, just respond to people's needs. God has been so good to us. What we are doing is just a drop in the ocean, but that ocean would be less without that drop.

—Mother Teresa, *A Simple Path*
(Ballantine, 1995)

The Miracle on 138th Street

For seven years, I served as Pastoral Associate and DRE at St. Mary of the Assumption Parish on 138th Street in Chicago. It is a small parish in a community with some big needs and big goals. One thing we wanted desperately to do was to add a service component to our religious education program. Our goal was to address the problem of hunger and poverty in the community. Who would take on such a challenge? How could we possibly feed and support so many people? Following the disciples' first line of thinking, perhaps it would be easier to send the people away. Yet Jesus spoke to us too: "*You* give them something to eat!"

After searching for a time for someone to coordinate the effort, a volunteer came forward to lead the project. A section in the rear of the church was dedicated as our "Caring Corner." Announcements went out to the children in religious education and to all parishioners who wanted to participate by donating cans of food for the food pantry. On the first Sunday of the project, I walked into the church to check on the "Caring Corner" table to see if anyone had brought a bag. To my amazement, I saw not only every inch of the table filled with bags of food, but every space on the floor surrounding the table filled as well. I was about to congratulate the coordinator when she said, "Come and see the usher's room!" My mouth dropped open as I peered into a room stacked from wall to wall with bags of canned goods! Not only did the fifty or so children in religious education take up the call to share what they had, but the parish as a whole got behind the project and took ownership of it. With each succeeding month, the miracle continued as baby clothes, pillows, blankets, and more canned goods came in to help those in need.

Jesus said to the parish, "*You* give them something to eat!" Someone answered that call and in no time a miracle of not-so-small proportions occurred on 138th Street in Chicago. A miracle like this is waiting to happen in your community. Jesus is speaking to you: "YOU give them something to eat!"

"Who Am I?" Checklist

Since Jesus is asking you to serve others, it might be a good idea to take inventory of yourself and affirm the gifts that Jesus sees in you. Place a check next to those qualities that best describe you:

I am . . .

___ Good	___ Compassionate	___ Giving
___ Dependable	___ Dedicated	___ Decisive
___ Sincere	___ Selfless	___ Loyal
___ Talented	___ Capable	___ Intelligent
___ Full of potential	___ In control	___ Outgoing
___ Pleasant	___ Warm	___ Deep
___ Interesting	___ Proactive	___ Consistent
___ Independent	___ Valued by others	___ Cooperative

Jesus is asking you to recognize the above gifts in yourself. How can these gifts help you to "feed" others?

Suggested Activities

- Have a chat with someone deeply involved in the ministry you are called to. Ask them how they felt when they were first asked to take on their ministry. What did they find difficult? What did they find rewarding?

- Go through your belongings and see what you can give away to others just to prove to yourself that you do have "food" for others.
- At the library, look up information about volunteer or service organizations (Peace Corps, Habitat for Humanity, etc.) and read up on the "miracles" that are occurring in the world today as a result of people saying "Yes!" to the call to serve others.

A Prayer for ME!

Lord, I usually prefer to pray for others! Yet, you've frightened me with these three letters by which you have recently called me: Y-O-U! I realize that people are in need of nourishment, but when I hear the words "*You* give them something to eat," I realize that I am responsible for my neighbor's well-being. Help me, Lord Jesus, to respond, "Here I am!" to your call. Strengthen me with your Holy Spirit so that I may give of myself to others.

Open my eyes to the miracles that are happening and will continue to happen when people like me hoist our sails and allow the strength of your Spirit to carry us to places where we can be of service to others. Let me humbly acknowledge the many gifts you have given me and, in turn, offer them back to you in service to your people. Like David, let me approach the "Goliaths" that stand before me with confidence knowing that you are always with me!

CHAPTER THREE

How Many Loaves Do You Have?

Assessing Your Resources

Feast or Famine?

Jesus asks, "How many loaves do you have?" Then he adds, "Go and see."

At this point it is clear that Jesus truly intends to feed the 5000 gathered guests. Despite the disciples' efforts to send the people away and avoid getting involved, Jesus begins discussing the menu! "How many loaves do you have?" Jesus asks. A quick inventory reveals the answer: five loaves and two fish. What kind of a meal can you make out of five loaves and two fish? The answer depends upon your perspective. You see, the disciples clearly thought that five loaves and two fish were not enough. In fact, you get the feeling that the disciples' report of the meager inventory was one more attempt to convince Jesus of the impossibility of the task at hand. Their hope was that Jesus would react by saying, "Oh well, in *that* case, perhaps you're right . . . let's send them away!"

No such luck.

To the disciples, five loaves and two fish seemed a paltry amount. To Jesus, it sounded like the beginnings of a feast!

Perspective

Successful ministry is all about perspective. Is the cup half full or half empty? Is it partly cloudy or partly sunny? Why is it that when two people look out through prison bars, one sees mud while the other sees stars? Perspective . . . that's the key.

Our perspective makes the difference between being reluctant and being willing. Our perspective makes the difference between staying on the sidelines and getting involved. Our perspective makes the difference between feeding people or sending them away. Depending on how we look at things, there will either be feast or famine.

For Reflection

- Who is someone you know who always seems to see things optimistically? How would this person view the challenge in ministry you currently face?
- Think of a time when the Lord provided for you even though it seemed like all you had were a few morsels of *possibility* to go up against 5000 *challenges*.

Using Your Imagination

Isn't Jesus out of touch with reality thinking that five loaves and two fish are enough to begin a feast with? Anyone with common sense can see 5 + 2 does *not* equal 5000! Is this a matter of perspective or insanity?

Jesus is, in fact, quite sane. All true leaders are. They just see differently. True leaders recognize reality as it is, but they do not stop there. True leaders see beyond reality to the realm of possibility. Jesus is not out of touch with reality but sees reality as full of possibilities. Throughout history, many great leaders have employed their imagination to see not only reality, but the potential that lies beyond. Like the disciples, Jesus saw 5000 hungry people. Like the disciples, Jesus saw a meager amount of food: five loaves and two fish. *Unlike* the disciples, Jesus had imagination enough to see the beginnings of a banquet!

In our own ministry, we may once again find ourselves like the disciples. A reality check suggests that we simply do not have the resources available to take on a new ministry. We do not have the time, the energy, the training, the manpower, or the financial resources to be successful. We only have five loaves and two fish. Surely Jesus will recognize that this is not sufficient for us to feed his people.

No such luck.

It seems that Jesus has a way of recognizing our limitations while at the same time seeing potential. Jesus possesses the type of imagination that lovers possess. Think about it. Did you ever look at a married couple that has been together for a long time and thought, "What do they see in each other after all these years?" It seems clear to you and everyone else that both people in question are obviously ordinary . . . yet they love each other as if they were more special than the finest king or queen. Are they out of touch with reality? Perhaps. But it is more than likely that, while they truly see each other's flaws, their love imaginatively allows them to recognize gifts and potential that are not so obvious to the rest of us. That's because love spawns imagination. Love has a way of helping us see beyond the limits of reality and into the realm of possibility.

Don't ever forget that Jesus loves you. He sees your flaws as plain as the nose on your face. But with his great love and imagination, Jesus also sees endless potential in you. He sees your five loaves and two fish, which you consider as meager, and thinks to himself: "Ah, the makings of another feast!" Jesus is inviting us to see as he sees: with a love that breeds imagination . . . recognizing reality and seeing beyond it to the realm of possibility.

For Reflection

- Who is a leader you know of with great imagination? Think of a time when this leader saw possibilities where everyone else saw none.
- What five loaves and two fish do you possess? In other words, what simple gifts do you possess that in Jesus' eyes may make the beginnings of a feast?
- Who is someone who believes that *you* possess great potential?

Developing a "Banquet" Mentality

What does it take to have a banquet? In short, abundance! A banquet or feast is basically a meal carried to the extreme. The food is in abundance. Decor is in abundance. Ambiance is in abundance. Everything is in abundance. Just what constitutes an abundance, however? Jesus shows us in the story of feeding the 5000 that abundance is a state of mind . . . a state of mind whose opposite is the mindset of scarcity. Abundance and scarcity are matters of perspective. The disciples, operating on a scarcity mindset, see five loaves and two fish as barely enough for an appetizer. Jesus, operating on a banquet or abundance mentality, sees the makings of a banquet.

In their book *A Passion for Excellence* (Warner Books, 1985), Tom Peters and Nancy Austin describe this phenomenon as the difference between what they call the "home run" mentality and the "Wee Willie Keeler" mentality. When we think of what it takes to get to the Baseball Hall of Fame, we think of Ruth, Gehrig, Mantle, Mays, and Aaron, all clobbering enormous numbers of home runs. "Wee Willie" Keeler made it to the Hall of Fame after hitting only thirty-four home runs in over twenty years. Lacking power, Keeler developed a mentality that said, "Hit 'em where they ain't." He could have chosen to perceive his lack of power as a drawback. Instead, Keeler resisted the scarcity mentality in favor of the abundance mentality and rode into the Hall of Fame on 2,955 hits that dropped in where the fielders weren't.

Dr. Wayne Dwyer, psychotherapist, lecturer, and author, says that to have a scarcity mentality means to

41

"evaluate our life in terms of its lacks." He says that "if we dwell on scarcity, we are putting our energy into what we do not have . . . and this continues to be our life experience." A banquet or abundance mentality, on the other hand, believes that "there is enough to go around, there is an endless universe to work in, and we are part of that endless universe," according to Dwyer. Abundance mentality sees five loaves and two fish as a plethora!

In our ministry, we often fall victim to the scarcity mentality that consumed the disciples instead of adapting the banquet mentality of Jesus. It is true that we face obstacles. It is true that our resources may indeed be limited. Anyone with common sense would agree. Imagination, however, is more powerful than common sense! Common sense (logic) suggests that the ministerial challenge you face cannot be achieved. The "Wee Willie Keeler" approach to ministry, on the other hand, suggests that you make do with what you have, adding up your small steps of success until you have something really big.

For Reflection

- What are some examples of small successes in your own ministry or the ministry of others that you have witnessed or participated in?
- In what way might you be trying to "hit a home run" in your ministry when a simple "base hit" or even a "sacrifice fly" will do for now?

Scripture for Prayer

But Mary said to the angel, "How can this be, since I have no relations with a man?" And the angel said to her in reply, "The holy Spirit will come upon you, and the power of the Most High will overshadow you. Therefore the child to be born will be called holy, the Son of God. And behold, Elizabeth, your relative, has also conceived a son in her old age, and this is the sixth month for her who was called barren; for nothing will be impossible for God."

—Luke 1:34-37

Jesus summoned the Twelve and gave them power and authority over all demons and to cure diseases, and he sent them to proclaim the kingdom of God and to heal the sick. He said to them, "Take nothing for the journey, neither walking stick, nor sack, nor food, nor money, and let no one take a second tunic. Whatever house you enter, stay there and leave from there. And as for those who do not welcome you, when you leave that town, shake the dust from your feet in testimony against them." Then they set out and went from village to village proclaiming the good news and curing diseases everywhere.

—Luke 9:1-6

Three times I begged the Lord about this, that it might leave me, but he said to me, "My grace is sufficient for you, for power is made perfect in weakness." I will rather boast most gladly of my weakness, in order that the power of Christ may dwell with me. Therefore, I am content with weaknesses, insults, hardships, persecutions, and constraints, for the sake of Christ; for when I am weak, then I am strong.

—2 Corinthians 12:8-10

"Do not be afraid," Elijah said to her. "Go and do as you propose, but first make me a little cake and bring it to me. Then you can prepare something for yourself and your son. For the Lord, the God of Israel says, 'The jar of flour shall not go empty, nor the jug of oil run dry, until the day when the Lord sends rain upon the earth." She left and did as Elijah had said. She was able to eat for a year, and he and her son as well; the jar of flour did not go empty, nor the jug of oil run dry, as the Lord had foretold through Elijah.

—1 Kings 17:13-16

In Their Own Words

The . . . biblical description of poverty is simplicity. People poor in this way are centered in chosen values instead of possessions. Few things are needed or desired by the one who lives simply because life is centered on another level of value. When Francis first heard Jesus' sermon in which he

44

told his followers to "take nothing for your journey," he left Mass overjoyed and committed the whole passage to memory, saying, "This is what I want. This is what I long for. This is what I desire to do with all my heart."

—Richard Rohr

The only difference between you and me is that you can see my handicap, but I can't see yours. We all have them. When people ask me how I've been able to overcome my physical handicaps, I tell them that I haven't overcome anything. I've simply learned what I can't do—such as play the piano or eat with chopsticks—but more importantly, I've learned what I can do. Then I do what I can with all my heart and soul.

—Roger Crawford

One of the most important decisions you can make to ensure your long-term happiness is to decide to use whatever life gives you in the moment. Success is the result of making small decisions; deciding to hold yourself to a higher standard, deciding to contribute, deciding to feed your mind rather than allowing the environment to control you . . . these small decisions create the life experience we call success.

—Anthony Robbins

Imagination, as I use the term, is not mental picture-making. It is neither make-believe nor fantasy. It is not meant as a way to avoid the real world, escaping to one's own desires and dreams. It is not a cop-out on reality. Rather, it is what Providence uses to get us deep down into the Real. Such knowing through the imagination is not irrational cognition and, therefore, false. It is not delusion. It is not a kind of knowledge against reason but rather a knowing that is beyond reason. What is disclosed to the imagination may be inconceivable, but it is not self-contradictory. It is simply more than meets the eye of mind or sense. Yet, it is indeed truth. It is not logic that leads to love, but imagination which discloses love's possibilities . . . possibilities that are more than meets the eye.

—Patrick Collins

In a final image, imagination is the room and thinking is the furniture. We may move the furniture from corner to corner to get new and fascinating looks. But sometimes what is needed is a larger room.

—John Shea

Poverty, Affirmation, and Innovation in Ministry

What does it take to minister with "meager" resources? Imagination! The key ingredients in imagination are a spirituality of poverty, a need for affirmation, and dedication to innovation.

46

The effective minister needs to practice a spirituality of poverty, a highly misunderstood concept in today's world. To practice poverty does not mean to punish oneself by denying any trappings of materialism. Rather, to practice poverty, one thankfully embraces that which he or she has to work with and sees it as wholly sufficient. True poverty in the spiritual sense means acknowledging that God's grace is enough. It means accepting five loaves and two fish as an abundance . . . a gift to be thankful for. It means avoiding the temptation to view things from a scarcity point of view in favor of a perspective of abundance. Those who practice true poverty, like Jesus, joyfully use what has been given to them. In our ministry, it means accepting what resources we have and using our imagination to transform scarcity into abundance.

An important element in this banquet mentality is the need for affirmation. As a minister, it is crucial that you find affirmation. Without affirmation, the scarcity mentality will prevail. Without affirmation, the minister begins to feel that he or she has little to offer. Without affirmation, imagination suffers. Affirmation, however, can be a tricky thing. If you have a superior who consistently affirms your work, you are very lucky . . . and possibly working on another planet! In my own experience as a pastoral associate, I have found that affirmation from the pastor and other staff members can be quite rare and sporadic. As a result, I developed a habit of affirming myself by letting the Lord affirm me in prayer. In the end, seeking affirmation from outside sources will prove to be fleeting. Rather than seeking affirmation from a variety of sources, accept it when it does come and continually allow the Lord the affirm you from within.

Finally, a minister that practices the spirituality of poverty and has a built-in sense of affirmation can become a master of innovation. Jesus was very innovative in finding a way to feed 5000 people with five loaves and two fish. He was able to do so because his spirituality of poverty told him to be thankful for what he was given to work with. He was successful because he felt the affirmation of his Father deep within telling him that he was indeed the Bread of Life. As a result, Jesus was able to be innovative. Simply put, innovation says to us, "Don't just stand there, do something!" The successful minister doesn't wait until he or she has an abundance of resources at hand. Instead, using the resources at hand, the successful minister innovates . . . does something . . . to begin addressing the needs at hand. Waiting for perfection to be achieved will mean waiting forever. Jesus may not have served the perfect bread and fish meal that day, but 5000 people went home satisfied.

Now you're being asked to serve a meal. Accept the resources given to you. Know that Jesus affirms your gifts. Use your imagination to innovate and begin feeding the hungry people of God who have come to you in search of good food.

The "I Think I Can . . . I Think I Can . . . I Think I Can . . ." Activity

Author Stephen Covey says that "Anytime we think the problem is 'out there,' that thought is the problem."

Use the following activity to stimulate an imaginative or innovative mindset rather than one that sees only problems and obstacles. The first sentences describe phrases often used by ministers that focus on problems "out there." Finish the second sentences to create statements that shift the focus to what you *can* do in spite of these realities.

"I would do this ministry if I had a bigger budget to work with."

"Even though I have a small budget, I can . . .

_____

_____

_____

"I would be a more effective minister if only my pastor/DRE/superior wasn't so stubborn."

"Even though my pastor/DRE/superior may sometimes be stubborn, I can . . .

_____

_____

_____

"If only I had more volunteers to assist me, my ministry would be much more successful."

"Even though I may not be surrounded by a good amount of volunteers, I can . . .

_____

_____

_____

"I cannot do this ministry without a degree."
"Even though I don't have a degree, I can . . .

_____

_____

_____

"I just don't have the same amount of time to pray the way I used to."
"While it's true that I have little time for myself, I still can . . .

_____

_____

_____

Suggested Activities

- Do the following activities to stimulate your imagination. First, "reinvent" the paper clip! In other words, come up with as many possibilities of new uses and purposes for the paper clip as you can. Next, brainstorm how you can improve the basic lead pencil. What would you do to make it a better instrument for what it is supposed to do? Be imaginative. Use these silly examples as an exercise in innovative thinking. Then, apply some of that innovation to your ministry.
- Conduct a "personal poverty inventory." In other words, look around your home or office and come up with a list of examples in which you have creatively used meager resources to make do. Example: the bookcase you created out of milk crates, the desk you've moved near the window for better lighting, the

older computer or software program you still use. Affirm yourself for your ability to do something with what you've been given. Begin to apply the same imagination to your ministry.

- Sit down and dialogue with someone who can genuinely affirm your giftedness, and you theirs. Take to heart all of the ways you have been affirmed and record it in a journal that you can go back and read when times are getting tough.

- Strive to be an optimist for one whole day. Remember, imagination does not mean being out of touch with reality but seeing beyond reality to potential. Don't look through rose-colored glasses, but truly try to find potential in any situation you find yourself in today. Record your thoughts at the end of the day and reflect upon how you can be a more optimistic and imaginative person. Apply this type of optimistic thinking to your ministerial challenges.

A Prayer for Imagination

Lord Jesus, help me to realize that your grace is all I need. You were able to begin a feast with five loaves and two fish. Help me to accept what resources you have given to me and to use my imagination to be truly innovative in ministry. Open my eyes to recognize the abundance that surrounds me. Dismiss the demons of scarcity and inspire me to adapt a banquet mentality. Help me to recognize the gifts you have given me and to use that affirmation to humbly serve others. In the same way,

51

grant that I may affirm others so that they in turn can find creative ways to share their loaves and fishes with others. Most of all, dear Lord, help me to *do something* to feed your people who hunger and thirst for justice, compassion, and mercy. Take my five loaves and two fish and prepare a banquet!

CHAPTER FOUR

The People Were Neatly Arranged

Organizing for Ministry

How Did We Do That?

Think back to some of the biggest events or accomplishments of your life: your wedding day, buying a new home, finishing your thesis, starting a new job, running a marathon. As each of those milestones occurred, you more than likely asked yourself whether you would really be able to pull it off. Now, as you look back, you probably ask yourself, "How did I ever do that?" Each day, we struggle to get out of bed and handle the mundane responsibilities and challenges of everyday life. How on earth did we find the energy to accomplish those major things?

How do you feed a crowd of 5000 people?

The answer is the same for both: by breaking down the big challenge into smaller challenges. Think again to one of your major milestones or accomplishments. The fact is, you didn't accomplish it all at one time. Little by little, you broke down the challenge into smaller ones. When you got married, you didn't wait for the wedding day to arrange for a hall, a church, a dress or tuxedo, a cake, a band, and a photographer. You accomplished these various tasks one at a time. You broke down the overwhelming concept of the "wedding day" into a series of smaller accomplishments leading up to the big day. When you wrote your thesis or dissertation, you didn't sit down on the day it was due and begin researching the topic before whipping off seventy-five typewritten pages. Rather, over the course of months or even years, you painstakingly gathered research and gradually wrote and rewrote your paper. When you ran the marathon, you didn't wake up one day and say, "I think I'll run twenty-six-plus miles today." The fact is, you began training months before, increasing your distance in increments until your body was prepared to handle the grueling marathon distance. The fact is, any major challenge is handled by breaking it down into smaller, more manageable parts.

Jesus did the same thing with 5000 people. After taking inventory and discovering all he had to work with was five loaves and two fish, he instructed his disciples to "make the people sit down on the green grass in groups or parties." The passage goes on to tell us that "The people took their places in hundreds and fifties." Now, instead of one group of 5000, they were looking at a number of smaller, more manageable groups.

Today, we call this "organizational development," and Jesus was a master of it.

Jesus broke down the overwhelming task of feeding 5000 people into the more manageable challenge of feeding groups of fifty to one hundred people. The question remains, "How *did* they eat?" Interestingly enough, the story doesn't really tell us. Nowhere does it tell us that Jesus waved his hand and instantly created mountains of food. In fact, nowhere in this story that we usually refer to as the "Multiplication of the Loaves and Fish" does it tell us that Jesus multiplied anything. Instead, it tells us that a large crowd was broken down into smaller groups and as the food was distributed, the people ate to their fill. So what was the miracle? The miracle is that somehow 5000 people fed each other! This was a faraway location. Obviously the people did not travel there without bringing some food for themselves. In smaller groups enough order and organization was established to allow people to reach into their own picnic baskets and willingly share what they had in the same way that Jesus and his disciples shared the five loaves and two fish they had.

This does not minimize the miraculous nature of this story or take anything away from Jesus' power. Rather, it takes it out of the realm of hocus-pocus and places it within a framework of reality so that we can continue to believe that Jesus can feed our crowds of 5000 in the same way he did nearly 2000 years ago! Through *organizational development* we, too, can facilitate gatherings of people that result in generous sharing of gifts and talents.

For Reflection

- What was a major accomplishment in your life? How did you break down the overwhelming challenge into smaller challenges that could be met one at a time?
- Think of someone who facilitates gatherings very effectively. What skills do they possess that allow them to assist a group of people in sharing their thoughts, gifts, talents, etc.? Which of these skills do you have? Which do you need to work on?

It's in the Details

When you go to a fine restaurant to dine, what impresses you? The hospitality? The decor and ambiance? The service? The food? The price? Most likely, all of the above! The finest restaurants are those that tend to all of the smallest details so that you can sit back and enjoy the meal.

In ministry, we are serving the finest food available: God's Word, the Body of Christ! As ministers, we are the *maitre d's*, the waiters and waitresses, the valets, the coat-checkers, and bus boys of Jesus' banquet. Our job as ministers is to tend to all of the details of any gathering that takes place in Jesus' name so that the sharing will result in a multiplication of resources. The church does not serve fast food! Rather, the church serves only the finest cuisine known to humankind. Jesus provides the food. We are called to tend to the details.

Think back to the story of the 5000. Jesus entrusted the disciples to take care of many details:

1. They had the people sit down on the green grass.
2. They organized parties of fifties or one hundreds.
3. They distributed the food.
4. They gathered the leftovers.

All of these details are part and parcel of the miracle. Details are the heart and soul of organizational development, a managerial concept that attempts to identify the "building blocks" of any group process or experience. These building blocks or details are then carefully tended to one at a time so that the end result is an effective gathering of people, a not-so-minor miracle in this day and age when people can't seem to agree on the smallest detail! By tending to all of the above mentioned details, the disciples played a very important part in the miracle of the loaves and fish. In fact, it seems that they did more of the nitty gritty work than Jesus!

Ordinary people tending to ordinary details so that the extraordinary may occur. That's what you're being called to! The bottom line in ministry is that we are being called to *set the table* for the finest meal money can't buy!

For Reflection

- When was the last time you hosted a large gathering of people for dinner at your house? Think of all the details that went into making the meal special. What went into "setting the table"?
- Think of a major parish or diocesan gathering (e.g., workshop, meeting, retreat) that you hosted or were a part of. What details needed to be tended to so that

those gathering could be properly "nourished"? What details were taken care of well? What details were overlooked?

Setting the Table for the Body of Christ

Every time we gather for Mass, our celebration is divided into two parts: the liturgy of the word and the liturgy of the eucharist. These two parts are separated by a small, unceremonious but very significant segment of the Mass referred to as the preparation of the gifts. This small part of the Mass should serve as a model for our ministry. In order for the Word of Life and the Bread of Life to connect, we need to set the table! In our ministry, through our "organizational development," as a result of tending to details, we ultimately set the table for Jesus to feed his people.

How do we do this?

Many of us are not comfortable with concepts such as *facilitating, organizational development,* or *group process.* So instead, we'll talk about "table-setting skills." Father Patrick Brennan says that his experience has shown that "What is needed in a small-group leader is not highly developed theological skills." Instead, he lists the following skills as more crucial for the effectiveness of the ordinary minister in terms of "setting the table":

- good body language for communication
- active listening
- how to ask informal questions
- how to ask open-ended questions that elicit life stories and faith sharing

- how to confront without putting another down
- empathy and the ability to communicate it
- affirming others
- drawing quiet persons out of the woodwork (those who want to come out)
- a comfort with silence
- a rehearsed flexibility . . . if what is prepared is not working
- a love of people
- a desire to be helpful rather than to impress
- the ability to handle anger, tears, hurt in self or in others
- the ability to gently redirect talkers who hold the group captive
- a growing ability to pray with others
- a relatively current knowledge of faith and church matters
- an ability to show humanity and vulnerability
- a willingness to share faith, when appropriate
- time both for ongoing training and support of fellow leaders
- a discipline to respect the agreed upon schedule and length of meetings
  —from *Re-Imagining the Parish* (Crossroad, 1991)

For Reflection

- Which of the "setting the table" skills are your strengths? Which do you need to improve upon? Who is someone who can help you improve at some of these skills?

These are skills that are within reach of those who are dedicated to setting the table for Jesus' extraordinary meals, namely, those gatherings that take place in his name whether they be RCIA sessions, catechist meetings, parish council meetings, Holy Name Society gatherings, a fifth-grade religion class, or a Women's Sodality luncheon. The same food is served at all of them: Jesus!

The story of the feeding of the 5000 provides a framework for four basic skills needed to set the table. Recall the four things that Jesus had his disciples do: seat the crowd, arrange groups, distribute the food, and collect the leftovers. These four actions provide every minister with a basic guide for ministry:

Seating the Crowd on the Grass		**Providing an Hospitable or Safe Climate**
Arranging Neatly in Groups		**Facilitating Interaction of Individuals**
Distributing the Food		**Carrying Out the Task**
Collecting the Leftovers		**Providing Closure and Evaluating**

Let's take a closer look at each of these.

Seat the Crowd on the Grass

In the story of the feeding of the 5000, we are told that the crowd had gathered in a "deserted place." A deserted place is not a very hospitable place for a picnic! In fact, the desert can be both dangerous and treacherous. The first order of business was to provide comfort and safety for the crowd. The story tells us that Jesus instructed the disciples to have the people seated on the *green grass*! No small trick in a deserted place! Yet, Jesus and his disciples located an environment that was both comfortable and safe for their guests: green grass in a deserted place.

Our first responsibility as ministers to God's people is to find a grassy place for them to be seated. Whenever people gather together in a group, it is as if gathering in the desert: the possibility of discomfort and danger are not lurking far away. Creating a climate that is hospitable and safe for God's people is crucial to the success of any gathering. Like a *maitre d'* at a fine restaurant, we must look to every detail of creature comfort to communicate to all those gathering that "you are welcome here and we want you to return over and over again." Hospitality involves everything from seating arrangements, comfort of chairs, and sightlines to tasty refreshments, sufficient supplies, and courtesy.

Likewise, people need to feel that the gathering itself is not threatening to them in any way. Many people find themselves feeling uneasy in group settings. It is the responsibility of the facilitator to ensure all present that their input is welcome (not forced) and respected. By paying attention to the details of hospitality and safety, we are providing God's people with a "grassy place" to be seated!

Arranged in Rows and Rows

Flowers in the desert? Yet the description of the people organized in rows of fifty and one hundred sounds a lot like a typical flower bed. In fact, earlier translations of this passage literally tell that the people were "neatly arranged like flower beds." Once again, the story presents images of growth and life (green grass and flower beds) in the midst of death (a deserted place). The disciples not only found a place where the 5000 could feel safe and comfortable, *they formed community!* In groups of fifty or one hundred, the people now resembled "flower beds" or collections of beautiful living organisms instead of a sea of confusion.

As ministers of Jesus' banquet, our next responsibility is to form community with those we serve by facilitating life-giving interaction. When people feel comfortable and safe, they will be much more willing to share their stories of faith and life experiences. In any gathering that we facilitate, we need to encourage communication and sharing: the two ingredients that form community and give life. Author Stephen B. Clark states in *Building Christian Communities* that "The main goal of the pastoral efforts in the church today is to build Christian communities which make it possible for a person to live a Christian life." He goes on to explain that such an environment is achieved "when a group of people interrelate or interact . . . in a consistent, regular way." When such an environment is formed, life grows and spreads like a bed of flowers.

Any gardener will tell you that it is the interaction of the soil, the moisture, the temperature, the sun, and the roots of the plants that allow flowers to flourish. As facilitators of a group, we are gardeners whose responsibility is to ensure the healthy interaction of individuals so that community is formed and life grows and spreads. Like the disciples, who neatly arranged the people in groups like flower beds, we, too, can form communities of life rooted in the love of Jesus.

Distribute the Food

A parishioner I once served used to spark the choir during lulls in the rehearsal by good-naturedly shouting, "Do something!" His point was always well taken: at some point you have to get down to business.

Now that the disciples have found a grassy place to sit and have neatly arranged groups like flower beds, they had to accomplish the goal of the gathering: distribute the food! Green grass and flower beds are nice but the bottom line was that people were hungry. However, I would like to think that it was *because* the first two steps were taken that the meal stretched as it did. With only five loaves and two fish in their arsenal, the disciples obviously did not have enough to feed the whole crowd. However, when people were made to feel at home, made to feel safe, made to feel part of a life-giving community . . . the food somehow became abundant! More than likely, people began to reach into their own baskets to share what little they had with their new neighbors. As the disciples distributed what little they had, it seems obvious that others came forward and said, "Here, you can distribute this as well!" The disciples' job was to see to the distribution of food. They carried out their task and somehow 5000 people ate to their fill.

Jesus told his disciples to distribute the food. Their goal was very clear, and they saw to it that the task was carried out. We, too, are called upon to *do something*! As ministers to God's people, we need to see to it that the main goal of any gathering is accomplished. Depending on our gathering, the goals will differ, but we must be clear what the goal of our gathering is so that we can see to it that it is carried out. As a facilitator of a Christian community, we must begin distributing the food and see to it that everyone has enough. The food being distributed, however, cannot all possibly come from us. Once we give away our five loaves and two fish, we must rely upon the food that is being generously offered by those in the group. By sticking to the goal of the gathering and facilitating the group's movement toward that goal, we are, in essence, seeing to it that the food is being distributed and that there is enough for all.

We are being called to *do something*! That "something" is to distribute the food, or in other words, carry out whatever task is needed to see to it that the Lord's people are truly fed and properly nourished.

Gather Up the Leftovers

I know that a meal is officially over when my wife brings out the Tupperware. It is at this point that we generally comment on how good (my wife's cooking is always good!) the meal was and when and how we will eat the leftovers. In one fell swoop, we evaluate the meal and plan the next one.

Jesus' disciples did the same thing. When the 5000 had eaten to their hearts' delight, the disciples went about and gathered enough leftovers to fill twelve baskets "besides what remained of the fish." I imagine that as the disciples went from group to group, the crowd offered comments about how nice the grassy area was, how fond they had become of the people in their groups, and how nicely bread and fish go together. Likewise, like any church gathering, I'm also sure that someone complained and offered suggestions for how this could be done better next time!

As ministers to the Lord's people, we, too, need to break out "Tupperware" to collect the leftovers from our gatherings. In other words, we need to provide closure for our gatherings and evaluate them so that we can improve upon the experience for next time. People need to know that *something* has been accomplished at any gathering. Closure does not mean that *all* of our work is done. It simply means that we are finished for this particular gathering until we meet again. By the same token, the most foolproof way to ensure that you will indeed have another meal at home is to save some leftovers. Likewise, the best way to ensure that your next gathering will have substance is to evaluate your present one and identify issues that need to be served up once again. Like any leftovers, you can be creative in how you disguise them to make them look and taste like a new dish next time around. Likewise, as you progress from one gathering to the next, you can become more and more creative in making sure that each one "tastes" different from the last.

By seating our people in a grassy area (providing an hospitable and safe environment), neatly arranging them in groups like flower beds (facilitating interaction and forming community), distributing the food (facilitating the group toward its goal), and gathering up the leftovers (providing closure and evaluating), we can feed God's people in the same way that Jesus fed 5000 with five loaves and two fish!

For Reflection

- Think of a gathering at which you and others felt uncomfortable or threatened. How could the facilitator have provided "green grass" (comfort and safety) for you and those attending? Likewise, think of a gathering at which you felt nothing was accomplished. How could the facilitator have better "distributed the food" (gotten the task done)?
- Think of a group experience in which isolated individuals formed a group. How long did it take? What was it that allowed the group to form community?
- Evaluate a gathering you recently attended or facilitated. What level of closure was achieved and how? What "leftovers" could be gathered up to provide for the next gathering? How could they be served in a new way?

Scripture for Prayer

In the beginning, when God created the heavens and the earth, the earth was a formless wasteland, and darkness covered the abyss, while a mighty wind swept over the waters. Then God said, "Let there be light," and there was light. God saw how good the light was. God then separated the light from the darkness. God called the light "day" and the darkness he called "night." Thus, evening came and morning followed—the first day.

—Genesis 1:1-5

So what is to be done, brothers? When you assemble, one has a psalm, another an instruction, a revelation, a tongue, or an interpretation. Everything should be done for building up. For you can all prophesy one by one, so that all may learn and all be encouraged. Indeed, the spirits of prophets are under the prophets' control, since he is not the God of disorder but of peace.

—1 Corinthians 14:26, 31-32

As they continued their journey he entered a village where a woman whose name was Martha welcomed him. She had a sister named Mary who sat beside the Lord at his feet listening to him speak. Martha, burdened with much serving, came to him and said, "Lord, do you not care that my sister has left me by myself to do the serving? Tell her to help me." The Lord said to her in reply, "Martha, Martha, you are anxious and worried about many things. There is need of only one thing. Mary has chosen the better part and it will not be taken from her."

—Luke 10:38-42

Be sure of this: if the master of the house had known the hour of night when the thief was coming, he would have stayed awake and not let his house be broken into. So too, you also must be prepared, for at an hour you do not expect, the Son of Man will come.

—Matthew 24:43-44

In Their Own Words

The little kindnesses and courtesies are so important. Small discourtesies, little unkindnesses, little forms of disrespect make large withdrawals. In relationships, the little things are the big things. I remember an evening I spent with two of my sons some years ago. In the middle of the movie, Sean, who was then four years old, fell asleep in his seat. His older brother, Stephen, who was six, stayed awake, and we watched the rest of the movie together. When it was over, I picked up Sean in my arms, carried him out to the car and laid him in the back seat. It was very cold that night, so I took off my coat and gently arranged it over and around him. When we arrived home, I quickly carried Sean in and tucked him into bed. After Stephen put on his "jammies" and brushed his teeth, I lay down next to him to talk about the night out together. There wasn't much response on his part. I found myself making conversation. I wondered why Stephen wouldn't open up more.

I sensed something was wrong. "What's wrong, honey? What is it?" "Daddy, if I were cold, would you put your coat around me, too?" Of all the events of that special night out together, the most important was a little act of kindness—a momentary, unconscious showing of love to his little brother. What a powerful, personal lesson that experience was to me then and is even now. People are very tender, very sensitive inside. I don't believe age or experience makes much difference. Inside, even within the most toughened and callused exteriors, are the tender feelings and emotions of the heart.

—Stephen Covey

Suggested Activities

- On a piece of paper, write down the name of a major project or challenge you are faced with. Underneath, draw a set of "building blocks." On each building block, write in a smaller accomplishment that will help you move a step closer to completing the whole project. Dedicate yourself to completing one small step at a time.
- Go out to eat at a nice restaurant. Make a mental "report card" listing and evaluating all of the amenities and services. Now, do the same for a church gathering of any kind. What kind of overall grade would you give the restaurant? The church gathering?

- Pull out some leftovers from your refrigerator and use your imagination to create a new and interesting meal. Keep this in mind when you carry business over from one parish gathering to another. Be creative and imaginative in coming back to the same "dish" with a little different flair.
- The next time you're on an elevator, ask yourself how it feels to be grouped with other strangers. This is how many people feel their first time at a church gathering! Try saying something on the elevator to break the ice. Use this episode to remind yourself to make groupings at your parish gatherings less intimidating and more inviting.

Setting the Table Checklist

Make a list below of all of the things you need to do ahead of time to set the table for your ministry (hospitality, supplies, etc.)

_____

_____

_____

_____

A Prayer for "Setting the Table"

Lord, when you came to eat dinner at the home of Martha and Mary, Martha complained about being left to tend to the details of hospitality. I sometimes feel like Martha! There is so much to do when people gather in your name, and I have to tend to so many details to make it comfortable, safe, hospitable, organized, and smooth. Help me to realize that these details need to be taken care of so that others can sit at your feet and listen to your word. Help me to realize that there are other "Marthas" out there who tend to the details occasionally so that I may take my turn at your feet. With the help of your disciples, you transformed a crowd of 5000 people into communities of sharing and faith and in doing so, fed them. Help me to tend to all of the details of setting the table for your banquets of love so that all who gather in your name will be nourished!

CHAPTER FIVE

They All Ate

Satisfying Hungers

Hungry? Hungry for What?

What was the best meal you ever had? What was so good about it?

Over the years, I've asked a number of people to reflect on these questions. What's interesting is that when most people describe the meal they're recalling, *they rarely describe the food*! In many cases, they do not even remember the food! Instead, they describe the people who were there, the laughter, the stories, an experience that occurred, singing, crying, hugging, sharing, and so on. Sure, the food was good, but other hungers were being fed . . . hungers more important than physical hunger. The fact is, people are hungry, not only for food, but for companionship, intimacy, trust, friendship, compassion, forgiveness, and joy. These are all hungers that cannot be satisfied by our society's "fast-food" mentality. The concept of fast food has left our society's hungers unsatisfied as more and more people eat alone and in a hurry.

Meanwhile, the people who come to us in our church settings are very hungry. Do we know what they are hungry for? Jesus once saw 5000 hungry people. Yet, he understood that they were hungry for much more than bread and fish. Jesus recognized that the crowd of 5000 had hungers that went beyond the physical. By forming communities of faith, Jesus was able to find the right kind of food to satisfy a variety of hungers . . . and the people ate their fill. Today, the people we serve are hungry. How do we feed them?

For Reflection

- What hungers do people in your ministerial setting need to have satisfied?
- What hungers has the Lord satisfied for you through the ministry of his church?
- What are you hungry for at this point in your spiritual life?

The Hunger to Be Known!

Recently, a church minister asked adults in his community what they needed most from the church in order to nourish their faith. They did not ask for small discussion groups. They did not ask for scripture study groups. They did not ask for prayer groups. Instead, they asked for dinner parties! They were hungry. But they weren't necessarily interested in food. They longed for the community that is formed when people gather around a table. When people gather around a table, no one is a stranger. The people in this parish wanted more than anything *to be known!* In much of society today, people are not known. On buses and trains, alone in our cars on congested expressways, in busy malls, and at fast-food restaurants, we are not known. We hunger to be known.

Despite meager resources, Jesus found the right food to feed 5000 people. It was the food that only a community of faith can provide. A miracle occurred and they all ate until they had their fill. They came to know one another and the Lord. The bottom line to the whole story is this: Bread is food that is meant to be shared. When food is shared, people are known to one another. Jesus is the Bread of Life. Jesus is the food that satisfies all hungers. He fed people then and he feeds people now, for in eating the Bread of Life, we come to know the Lord and one another!

The people of God continue to hunger for more of this food. Jesus has given us all the ingredients we need to create some interesting recipes. In Christian communities all over the world (perhaps even your own), disciples of Jesus are creatively feeding the people of God. Let's take a look at a variety of creative recipes that have fed many a hungry crowd despite seemingly meager resources.

The Do-It-Yourself Approach

What happens when you can't find a qualified presenter for your adult education program, or you don't have a budget to pay someone to come in, or your speaker cancels and you're left with a void in your program? One parish staff found themselves in just such a quandary when looking at their upcoming lenten program. The speaker they had sought was unavailable and last minute substitutes were not working. Finally, they came up with the idea of inviting parishioners to share their own personal faith stories! Instead of an "expert" coming in to lecture or give a presentation, a panel of parishioners was gathered each week to reflect and share stories from their life experience based on the theme of the upcoming Sunday scripture readings. The resulting format, like a parish "talk-show," was overwhelming. A lenten program that once attracted twenty-five to thirty parishioners doubled in size as people found out that their own friends and neighbors were witnessing to the power of the Lord in their lives!

A high school administrative team likewise found a similar solution for their faculty retreat for which a speaker canceled. After unsuccessfully pursuing some last minute replacements, the staff came up with the idea of asking faculty members to give the retreat themselves. Panels of faculty members were put together based on a variety of themes concerning their teaching experience as related to their faith. The success of this makeshift retreat resulted in a permanent change in their retreat plans: from then on the faculty retreat was given by the faculty. Teachers eagerly awaited the opportunity to see their colleagues open up and share their faith as well as the opportunity to do so themselves. They found it refreshing to talk to each other about Jesus for once instead of biology, social studies, discipline, or curriculum. They found enough food to feed one another!

The <u>Don't</u> Do-It-Yourself Method

Several small parishes found themselves struggling to provide catechist formation for their own small groups of catechists at their respective parishes. Likewise, their catechists found it difficult to travel to the programs offered by the archdiocese. The DREs found it difficult to prepare full-fledged catechist formation programs for the small number of catechists who could or would attend. After sharing their frustrations, the DREs decided to pool their resources and offer a regional catechetical formation program that would offer programming at each parish on a rotating basis. Another obstacle to be overcome was the lack of any budget to draw in speakers to facilitate the sessions. Instead, the DREs decided to take on the responsibility of facilitating the sessions themselves. The result was the establishment of a quality program that was convenient for catechists to attend. Likewise, although each parish still sent a small number of catechists to each gathering, the combined numbers made for animated sharing of experiences. Catechists enjoyed the opportunity to meet their colleagues from the neighboring parishes and compare notes and stories. The success of the idea resulted in its growing from one gathering per year to a quarterly gathering culminating in an appreciation dinner for the catechists of all the parishes involved. What began as frustration over meager resources (five loaves and two fish) resulted in a regional banquet of catechetical ministers!

Feeding Our Youth

"We need to do more for our youth!" This refrain is very familiar in many of our churches . . . and deservedly so. Quality youth programs in Catholic churches tend to be the exception to the rule, and as a result, youth are often going hungry for spiritual nourishment. One parish struggled to offer more for their youth only to be frustrated by the perennial problems of low turnout and financial constraints. The parish could not afford a youth minister for the ten to twelve teens who were consistently participating and looking for more nourishment. Instead of folding up shop and telling the kids to come back when they are married and have children of their own, the church tried an innovative solution. As it turned out, the Baptist church a mile or two down the road was experiencing the same problems. Leaders from both churches put their heads together and decided to recruit some volunteers to host an occasional combined gathering for all of their teens, many of whom went to the same high school. Instead of ten to twelve teens gathering at their respective churches, now there were twenty to thirty getting together at each other's churches on a rotating basis, allowing for more activities and greater socializing under the supervision of volunteers from each church. In between these gatherings, each church continued to gather their youth at their own church for continued formation in their own tradition. However, the youth no longer felt alone and isolated. Together with the adults, they gained a valuable lesson in ecumenism while at the same time each church was able to provide some much needed nourishment for young people who otherwise would have gone away hungry!

Mystagogia Meals

Many people who work in the adult catechumenate (RCIA) for the first time find the post-Easter period to be somewhat vague and frustrating. "What do we do now that they have received the sacraments?" Staff members from several parishes got together and shared their quandary over how to best "do" the mystagogia ("pondering the mysteries of faith") period following Easter. Once again, they felt as though they had little or no food to satisfy the hunger of their crowds. Then came a breakthrough! They decided to invite all of their neophytes to gather together in one location to share their stories of their catechumenate journey, the Easter Vigil, and their hopes for the future. Thirty neophytes and catechumenate team members from five parishes gathered together for what turned out to be an evening of prayer, praise, and sharing of stories. Neophytes who had been quiet and shy throughout their catechumenate suddenly found the courage to share out loud as they compared notes with their brothers and sisters from the other parishes. Team members were nourished by the telling of innovative and creative approaches to doing the catechumenate process. The gathering ended in an agreement to meet several more times, to visit each other's churches, and to continue sharing stories of their faith development and new life in Jesus, the Bread of Life!

Learning from the Masters . . .

A veteran catechist was disappointed to learn that the DRE she admired and looked up to was moving to another city. Her disappointment turned to shock when the pastor approached *her* and asked her to consider becoming the new DRE! After much thought and prayer, she accepted the position and, with much fear and trepidation, came in to the parish office to begin her work. Her first move was to call the diocesan office of catechetical ministry and ask for help! Wisely, she realized that there were many seasoned DREs out there who could be of help to her. She requested that the diocesan office locate a mentor for her, someone in a similar situation as hers but a few years ahead so that she could learn from the wisdom of experience. From time to time, she was able to get together with her mentor and share the joys and frustrations of the job as well as the spiritual graces of being a catechetical leader. Jesus did not feed the 5000 alone; he counted on the help of his disciples. This new DRE was wise enough to do the same!

Give Them Something to Eat . . . Literally!

Many parishes struggle with the small turnouts at adult education gatherings. Pastoral ministers often feel that they are unable to entice people to come out and "taste and see" the nourishment the gospel can offer. One parish discovered that the best way to feed people's souls was to feed their stomachs first! Every adult education event got connected to a meal of some kind! A monthly

Sunday theology presentation became attached to a delicious breakfast catered by a local restaurant. Attendees covered the cost of their meals and the crowds went from about fifteen to fifty. Likewise, the same parish doubled the size of their lenten mission attendance by offering a soup and bread meal to go with the presentation. Families gave up their regular meal at home to come and join in a simple lenten meal and to socialize with others. Free will donations covered the cost of the soup and bread. People weren't as hungry for the meals as they were to be known, something that happens when they join others at table. Finally, each weekend after the Masses, the parish hosted a "Coffee and . . ." reception in the parish hall with parishioners taking turns donating coffee, juice, and doughnuts. Each week, new and old parishioners gathered for fellowship. A parish that once felt like a large disconnected crowd now felt like they had been neatly arranged as if rows in a flower bed. Sometimes, it seems, the best way to feed people's hunger is to literally feed them!

Stop the Insanity!

A contemporary definition of insanity is the act of doing the same thing over and over again while expecting different results! For example, if a child said he or she absolutely detested Brussels sprouts, it wouldn't make much sense to serve him or her Brussels sprouts every day hoping that one day he or she will say, "Hey, I like these!" Yet, in ministry, we often perform a variation of this same madness. We offer the same stale programs over and over again and wonder why no one seems interested. Year after year, we get frustrated that very few people are taking advantage of the "food" we are serving in our parishes and end up borrowing a line from Chicago Cub fans: "wait until next year!" Unfortunately, when next year comes around, we are serving pretty much the same Brussels sprouts and fielding basically the same team that lost last year.

One parish decided to change all this. Year after year saw a steady decline in the number of people attending a traditional scripture study until the group had dwindled to only two or three. The parish leaders tried changing the time. They tried changing the day. They tried changing the location. Finally, the parish staff decided to change the whole concept of how to do scripture study. Previously, they invited people to gather and focus on a particular book of the Bible and share some reflection questions on it. Now, instead of focusing primarily on the text, the staff decided the gatherings should focus on life! A new Bible and faith sharing gathering was offered in which experiences, issues, and topics from daily life were shared and then reflected upon in light of biblical passages. Instead of inviting people to come out to discuss Exodus, Corinthians, or Isaiah, the parish was now inviting people to come and discuss communication in relationships, dealing with difficult people, faith in the workplace, managing your time, and more, all within a biblical context. Participants began by sharing stories of their experience of daily living based on a selected theme or topic. A facilitator provided selected scripture passages to provide a biblical context. In addition to these previously selected passages, many participants came prepared to share their own favorite passages and expound upon them. The two or three people previously attending multiplied until more chairs were needed for a room that held about thirty! Instead of serving the same tired leftovers over and over again, this parish staff decided to cook up a new recipe. Not only did the "meal" grow in numbers, but people were "reaching into their baskets" to share the wisdom and experience of their lives and in doing so, fed one another.

Where Two or Three (Parishes) Are Gathered

Three neighboring inner-city parishes each struggled without their own qualified director of religious education due to lack of financial resources. No one parish could afford to hire a full-time professional to address the catechetical needs of their own parish, let alone the entire area. With the assistance of the diocesan catechetical office, the three parishes pulled together to apply for and secure a grant that allowed them to hire a tri-parish director of religious education for a period of three years. The professional catechetical leader who was hired to serve the three parishes was able to mobilize a dedicated crew of volunteer catechetical ministers at each of the three sites and orchestrate them in a coordinated manner. Following the three-year grant, the parishes committed to continuing the arrangement for at least another three years with resources from all three parishes combined to sustain the salary of the tri-parish DRE. Thus, by following the biblical wisdom that says, "Where two or three gather in my name there I am in your midst," these parishes gathered together to help the people of God recognize the Bread of Life present in their midst through the catechetical ministry.

For Reflection

- From your own experience, what are some examples of people being fed despite meager resources?
- Where do you presently see a need for people to be fed despite meager resources? What can be done?
- When were you once fed in a situation that seemed hopeless?

Scripture for Prayer

Here in the desert, the whole Israelite community grumbled against Moses and Aaron. The Israelites said to them, "Would that we had died at the Lord's hand in the land of Egypt as we sat by our fleshpots and ate our fill of bread! But you had to lead us into this desert to make the whole community die of famine!" Then the Lord said to Moses, "I will now rain down bread from heaven for you." In the evening quail came up and covered the camp. In the morning, a dew lay all about the camp and when the dew evaporated, there on the surface of the desert were fine flakes like hoarfrost on the ground. On seeing it, the Israelites asked one another, "What is this?" Moses told them, "This is the bread which the Lord has given you to eat."

—Exodus 16:2-4, 13-15

When they climbed out on shore, they saw a charcoal fire with fish on it and bread. Jesus said to them, "Bring some of the fish you just caught." So Simon Peter went over and dragged the net ashore full of one hundred fifty-three large fish. Even though there were so many, the net was not torn. Jesus said to them, "Come, have breakfast." And none of the disciples dared to ask him, "Who are you?" because they realized it was the Lord.

—John 21:9-12

And it happened that, while he was with them at table, he took bread, said the blessing, broke it, and gave it to them. With that their eyes were opened and they recognized him, but he vanished from their sight. Then they said to each other, "Were not our hearts burning within us while he spoke to us on the way and opened the scriptures to us?" So they set out at once and returned to Jerusalem where they found gathered together the eleven and those with them who were saying, "The Lord has truly been raised and has appeared to Simon!" Then the two recounted what had taken place on the way and how he was made known to them in the breaking of the bread.

—Luke 24:30-33, 35

Jesus said to them, "I am the bread of life; whoever comes to me will never hunger, and whoever believes in me will never thirst. I am the bread of life. Your ancestors ate the manna in the desert, but they died; this is the bread that comes down from heaven so that one may eat it and not die. I am the living bread that came down from heaven; whoever eats this bread will live forever; and the bread that I will give is my flesh for the life of the world."

—John 6:35, 48-51

In Their Own Words

Jean Vanier, the Canadian who founded a worldwide network of communities for mentally disabled people, has remarked more than once that Jesus did not say: "Blessed are those who care for the poor," but, "Blessed are the poor." Simple as this remark may seem, it offers the key to the kingdom. I want to help. I want to do something for people in need. I want to offer consolation to those who are in grief and alleviate the suffering of those who are in pain. There is obviously nothing wrong with that desire. It is a noble and grace-filled desire. But unless I realize that God's blessing is coming to me from those I want to serve, my help will be short-lived, and soon I will be "burned out." How is it possible to keep caring for the poor when the poor only get poorer? How is it possible to keep nursing the sick then they are not getting better? How can I keep consoling the dying when their deaths only bring me more grief? The answer is that they all hold a blessing for me, a blessing that I need to receive. Once I asked Jean Vanier: "How do you find the strength to see so many people each day and listen to their many problems and pains?" He gently smiled and said: "They show me Jesus and give me life." Here lies the great mystery of Christian service. Those who serve Jesus in the poor will be fed by him whom they serve: "He will put on an apron, set them down at table and wait on them" (Lk 12:37).

—Henri Nouwen

I Only Have Five Loaves and Two Fish!

Most people think that they have only five loaves and two fish. In others words, when it comes to feeding others, the average parishioner feels that he or she has very little to offer. We tend to think that only those with a certificate, a credential, a diploma, or an ordained office can provide nourishment for others. Like John the Baptist, most of us remark, "I should be baptized (fed) by you, yet you come to *me!?*" While professionalism is crucial for church leadership, recall that the disciples did not have M.Divs or D.Mins or any initials after their names, and yet they somehow participated in the feeding of 5000 people! While our credentialed and ordained leaders are called to mobilize the troops, *we* are being called to share the loaves and fish that we have stored in our baskets. In my experience, I have had people who said, "No, you can't mean me . . . what do I have to offer?" turn out to be RCIA team members, first communion catechists, leaders of song, scripture study facilitators, family life ministers, and more. All because they reached into their basket, found some food, and shared it with others!

Bread is the food of hospitality. It is food that is meant to be shared. When we pray, "Give us this day our daily bread," we are asking the Lord to give us what we need to share with others. The bread we receive is not meant for ourselves. As Jesus offers us his own flesh, the Bread of Life, he is saying, "Here . . . give *them* something to eat!"

Rest assured, with food like this, we will *all* eat until we have our fill!

Suggested Activities

- Observe the people eating in a fastfood restaurant. Look into their faces. What hungers do you see that are going unfed?
- Think about the three biggest meal-occasions you celebrated during the past year (e.g., a wedding, an awards banquet, etc.). Make a mental list of the people who were present and what you talked about. Now, try to recall the menu that was served at each meal. Which was easier to remember, the people or the food?
- Find a mentor or colleague with whom you can combine resources to accomplish the ministry you are about to engage in. Discuss how you can more effectively feed people's hungers by pooling resources.
- Conduct a survey of what people really want most from their church. Leave it open-ended to allow people to creatively express what they really want (as opposed to

selecting "churchy" programs, e.g., "prayer groups" etc.). Even if answers seem far-fetched (one parish group responded by requesting a trip to a hot tub!), try to discern what hungers they truly have (what they are really asking for) and how the church can provide nourishment.

Hunger Checklist

Place a check next to the hungers that are most prevalent among the people you minister to:

___ compassion	___ love	___ attention	___ forgiveness
___ knowledge	___ intimacy	___ faith	___ justice
___ friendship	___ trust	___ joy	___ comfort
___ other			

A Prayer for Daily Bread

Jesus, you are the Bread of Life! You have nourished me in so many ways. I know now that bread is meant to be shared, for it is the food of hospitality. More than ever, Lord, I pray that you give us this day our daily bread, not so that I may eat and be nourished but so that I may have enough to share with others. Your people are hungry, Lord. We are in need of nourishment. We hunger for justice, mercy, companionship, joy, consolation, comfort, healing, forgiveness, intimacy, and so much more. You alone are the Bread of Life. You alone satisfy the hungry heart. As I pray in the words you gave us, Lord, help me to remember that "our daily bread" is meant to be given away so that others may know that *you* are the Bread of Life!

CHAPTER SIX

They Gathered Up Leftovers

Closure in an Ongoing Ministry

Ministerial "Tupperware"

Personally, I like leftovers. At the end of every meal, I pull out my trusty Tupperware containers and diligently store all of the mashed potatoes, corn, gravy, vegetables, and meat in the refrigerator. The next day, I have lunch all set to be microwaved and occasionally there is enough left over for the whole family to make a hodgepodge for dinner! By the same token, it unfortunately happens that my leftovers get buried deep in the refrigerator and are eventually forgotten. After a couple of weeks, they are discovered only to be tossed out due to spoilage. What a waste.

In the feeding of the 5000 we learn that the disciples collected leftovers . . . twelve wicker baskets full. When a meal is prepared properly, there will always be more than enough to go around. In our ministry, as we participate in nourishing God's people, we, too, need to be aware of the "leftovers" that will result whenever people gather in Jesus' name. When people gather in the name of the Lord, Jesus nourishes and satisfies with such abundance that there will always be something left over. As ministers, we need to be aware of what we mean by left overs, how to "collect" and "store" them, and how to avoid allowing leftovers to "spoil" or become forgotten.

All too often, the ideas and energy that are left over at a gathering of God's people are either not "packed up" for future use, or they are stored away in a file, only to be forgotten. As disciples of Jesus, we not only set the table for the banquet, we also have the responsibility of collecting and storing the leftovers for future nourishment.

What's a Leftover?

When you finish a meal, you can easily decide what should be saved and what should be discarded. Some portions are too small and *should* be discarded. Likewise, some scraps are too paltry to save. However, some portions are large enough to serve a whole other meal while other scraps are left over in such a quantity and variety that they can be creatively recycled in a brand new meal!

What is left over after the people of God gather? Like any meal, if it was prepared properly, there will be a certain amount of leftovers such as energy, ideas, unfinished business, and more. One gathering of God's people will produce an abundance of nourishment that will lead to future gatherings.

No one meal can possibly satisfy one's hunger for a lifetime. By the same token, no one gathering of the people of God can satisfy all of the spiritual hungers brought to the table. As disciples of Jesus, we need to be aware of what can be collected from one gathering to store and preserve for future gatherings so that nothing is wasted and the people are never left unfed.

But I Don't Like Leftovers!

To some people, the idea of leftovers sounds depressing. Leftovers can grow stale, tiresome, and boring. Leftovers can lose their flavor and crispness. In ministry, if all we serve are leftovers, we will not properly nourish God's people. All too often, churches fall into the habit of serving up the same menu of tired leftover programs and activities. Like a family eating turkey for weeks after Thanksgiving, we long for something fresh and new.

In our treatment of the idea of collecting and saving leftovers, we are not talking about doing the same old thing over and over again. Instead, we are referring to the common sense and wisdom that is needed to preserve that which retains flavor and nourishment for God's people and should not be wasted. Jesus will always continue to provide us with fresh nourishment, but we must not let his abundance go to waste. Like any good parent feeding a family, we must strike a balance between leftovers and new ideas. Likewise, we need to be creative in serving leftovers so that they don't look or taste like the same old thing!

For Reflection

- What is your attitude toward leftovers? In what ways do you preserve and creatively use leftovers for future meals?
- What do you think is "leftover" whenever the people of God gather?

What Are the Twelve Baskets of Leftovers?

The story of the Feeding of the 5000 tells us that enough scraps were collected to fill twelve baskets! Why twelve? First of all, it is important to notice that biblical authors used numbers for their symbolic value. Certain numbers pop up over and over in the scriptures. Like:

- Forty (It rained forty days and forty nights for Noah; the Israelites wandered the desert for forty years; Jesus spent forty days in the desert; etc.)
- Three (Moses spent three days on the mountaintop before returning with the commandments; Jonah spent three days in the whale; Jesus spent three days in the tomb; etc.)
- Twelve (There were twelve tribes of Israel; twelve apostles; twelve thousand saved from the twelve tribes in the Book of Revelation; etc.)

The repeated usage of these numbers indicates to us that they are meant to convey something symbolic. Forty conveys a period of significance, often associated with preparation or repentance. The third day is always the day upon which salvation occurs. The number twelve represents completeness or fullness. The twelve tribes of Israel represent all of the people of Israel. The twelve apostles represent the fullness of discipleship. The 144,000 (a multiple of twelve!) who are saved in Revelation represent all of those who will be saved.

It is no accident that the disciples collect enough scraps to fill twelve baskets!

In this case, we can conclude that all of Jesus' disciples (including us) will have an abundance if we come to him for nourishment and work with him to set the table. The message for us is that when people gather in Jesus' name and conspire with the Spirit to set the table for the banquet, there will be an abundance . . . so much so that there will be enough left over to be collected, organized, and preserved for future use!

Since twelve is a symbolic number, let's use our imaginations to fill these twelve baskets with the leftovers that result from any gathering of God's people. Let's get a better idea of what we can hope to see an abundance of whenever we gather God's people together for nourishment. What can we fill our twelve baskets with that will serve us in ministry?

Basket #1: Ideas

Anytime the people of God gather together under the inspiration of the Holy Spirit, ideas start to fly. "What if . . . ?" "Why don't we . . . ?" "Next time, let's . . . !" Quite often, many of these ideas are constructive and helpful for the task at hand. Sometimes, ideas are suggested that cannot be dealt with at the present time, much in the same way not all of the food at a meal can be consumed. The important thing to remember is to *always* have a place to "put" these ideas. As ministers, we should never tell someone who is volunteering an idea that there is no room for them! We would never turn away someone coming to our door with a gift of food! Even if we have just eaten, we will accept it and store it. Ideas that can be worked on immediately should be dealt with promptly. Ideas whose time or place needs to be determined should be accepted, recorded, and placed somewhere they will not be forgotten. (As a DRE, I kept a "Wait Till Next Year" file for any ideas that came up that could not be implemented in the current year.) Whatever the case may be, we need to be sure to go back and retrieve what has been stored lest it be forgotten and spoil.

Basket #2: Energy

Whenever the Spirit is released upon a group of people gathered in Jesus' name, energy is abundant! One of the leftovers that needs to be preserved is the energy that is created and freely flowing from a gathering of God's people. Energy is preserved by spreading the news of successful gatherings, telling the story, capturing and displaying photographs, inviting absentees to attend what they missed, and sending out participants as "ambassadors" to carry out tasks and invite newcomers. Energy is preserved by directing it outward instead of keeping it to ourselves. If we selfishly hoard the energy of the Spirit, it dies. At the same time, if we save food from a meal without deciding when that next meal will occur, the food will go to waste. When energy is preserved from one gathering, it needs to be directed toward the next step, the next gathering of the assembly, so that it can not only be sustained, but continue to build and produce a snowball effect.

Basket #3: Fellowship

Many long-lasting relationships are formed from church gatherings. (My wife and I met at a church gathering. I guess she got the leftovers!) When we gather in the Lord's name and are nourished by the Bread of Life, we forge relationships with one another in the same way that people do when they go out to eat with one another. Jesus took advantage of every opportunity to join others at meals, not because he loved food so much, but because he knew that to eat a meal with another person was to enter into covenant with them. As we gather people together in the name of the Lord, we need to focus on establishing relationships. Fellowship is not a fluffy extra . . . it is a basic human hunger. Some of the leftovers we need to foster, nourish, and preserve are the relationships that are established at church gatherings. As leaders of church gatherings, WE ourselves establish new relationships that will nourish us beyond the scope of this particular gathering. Likewise, we bring others into relationship with one another. Fellowship that is preserved will provide the basis for growth, especially if it is always outward moving and welcoming, not turned in on itself. If we do not focus our attention on the need to feed the hunger for fellowship, we might as well become a fast-food restaurant!

Basket #4: New Disciples

Remember how we said that some leftovers can be combined creatively to create a whole new dish to serve? In the same way, when we establish fellowship and get to know one another, we discover something wonderful: new disciples of Christ! Quite often, people are waiting to be invited to share their gifts with the community of believers, but because fellowship is often ignored, the gifts of these individuals go unnoticed. When we take the time to get to know people and for them to get to know one another, we realize that we are talking to musicians, teachers, business people, executives, doctors, parents, and grandparents who may be willing to share their time, talent, and treasure in service of the body of Christ. Some of the most valuable leftovers of any Christian gathering are the persons who show interest in moving to the next step in their relationship with Jesus and the church. Maybe you yourself will not be able to put their talents to work in the ministry you are engaged in, but, like taking leftovers to your neighbor's house, you can identify their gifts and introduce them to someone who can.

Basket #5: Special Needs

Sometimes at the end of a meal, certain leftovers need to get special treatment in order to be saved: the rest of the ham or turkey needs to be carved in order to fit in the refrigerator; the dairy products need to be stored quickly lest they spoil, certain foods need to be frozen, etc. In much the same way, at many church gatherings, we come face to face with people who have special needs that need to be tended to right away: the single mother who is courageously struggling to take care of her family on her own; the couple going through the death of a child; the middle-aged man who is coping with the loss of his job as a result of down-sizing; the father who has been away from the church for a number of years. These leftovers must be dealt with immediately. Again, you yourself may not be capable of dealing directly with all of these needs yourself, but as pastoral ministers, we need to be ready to show care and compassion to those in need. Like the disciples gathering up leftovers after the feeding of the 5000, we need to be aware of the fact that one of the leftovers we will encounter at any church gathering are those special ones that need immediate and preferential attention.

Basket #6: The Establishment of Rituals

Think back to a time when you and a friend or group of friends went out and had the most unbelievably good time: the place or places you went, the crazy and wonderful things you did, the stories, jokes, and laughter you shared, and the food you ate were all part of this wonderful experience. No doubt, when you gathered once again with this friend or group of friends, you sought to re-create the experience and recapture the feeling of that special time together. When we do the same thing(s) over and over again to re-create or recapture the essence of a previous experience, we establish ritual. Whenever the people of God gather and discover nourishment in Jesus and fellowship in one another, the desire to re-create or recapture that nourishment once again will be unavoidable. While each gathering is unique and fresh, we can still isolate certain ingredients of that initial gathering that were responsible for creating the "magic" and develop them into rituals to be preserved for future gatherings. Perhaps it was the seating arrangement, the lighting, the icebreaking activities, the prayer experience, the food, the depth of sharing, the mutual trust, the level of enthusiasm, or a combination of some or all of the above. Whatever the case, those "ingredients" that contributed to the success of a gathering may serve as the beginnings of future rituals, for example, they may be preserved and re-created, repeated, or recaptured over and over again at future gatherings in order to continue to provide the nourishment they did with the same freshness they originally had.

Basket #7: Evaluation

When the disciples collected the scraps that filled the baskets, I'm sure they scrutinized what they were saving. Some things were worth keeping while others were not. This type of evaluation goes on anytime we are collecting leftovers. By the same token, decisions can be made based on this evaluation. If the disciples collected twelve baskets of leftover bread and no fish, perhaps they would tell Jesus, "Next time, more fish and less bread!" In much the same way, as we sort through the aftermath of our gatherings, we must recognize the importance of the basket known as evaluation. To paraphrase a famous saying, "The unevaluated ministry is not worth serving in!" All of our ministries, whether we are doing them for the first time or the one thousand and first time, must be evaluated! Through the process of evaluation, we come to recognize which hungers are being fed and how. At the same time, we learn how we can better nourish those we are serving and recognize hungers that are yet to be fed. When the Lord feeds us, we need to pay particular attention to what role we and others played in setting the table so that we can improve upon our stewardship of God's people.

Basket #8: Charity

One of the most beloved hymns of Christian tradition is "Ubi Caritas" with it's wonderful refrain of "Where charity and love prevail, there God is ever found!" God is found whenever two or three gather in Jesus' name, so it is safe to say that charity should be an abundant leftover of any Christian gathering! In any ministry we participate in, charity toward others must be a standard ingredient, whether it be charity toward those we are gathering with or charity directed to a target audience or cause beyond our gathering. If charity is not found in abundance at Christian gatherings, then we must begin to question just how Christian our gathering is. It is quite possible that the true miracle of the feeding of the 5000 was the charity the crowd displayed toward one another in sharing what little they had to the extent that twelve baskets of leftovers were collected. If our ministry is truly open to the Holy Spirit, we, too, will discover an abundance of charity left over to be collected and distributed to those who need it most.

Basket #9: Unfinished Business

No one meal will satisfy our hunger forever. We will always need to eat another meal. In the same way, it is impossible to complete all of the business of the gospel at any one gathering of God's people. No matter how efficient we may be, there will always be more work to be done. *Every gathering of God's people will result in unfinished business.* As much as we may try to tie up all the loose ends and make a nice package of the reality we call ministry, we will never be finished with the work of the gospel. The sooner we realize that one thing will always lead to another, the less frustrated we will be that our work never seems to get done. It never will! Instead of approaching unfinished business as though it were more work to be done, we should think of it as leftover nourishment for a future meal. We don't get angry at the thought of having leftover food because we know that we will always have to eat again. Yet, for some reason, we get stressed out when it appears that we have unfinished business in our ministry. By its very nature, the gospel is unfinished business! The author of Mark's gospel knew this and originally ended the gospel in chapter 16, verse 8 with the women fleeing the empty tomb in fear. No happy ending. No closure. Just the sense of an unfinished story. (Only later did editors tack on other endings to provide more closure.) In the same way, the gospel of Mark starts off very appropriately in chapter 1, verse 1: *"Here* begins the Good News of Jesus Christ!" The gospel is not concerned with endings but beginnings! We too should not be concerned about unfinished business but with the fact that every time we gather in Jesus' name, the good news of Jesus begins again!

Basket #10: Closure

While we should never allow unfinished business to overwhelm us, at the same time, we should not allow it to trail off into oblivion. Unfinished business, like quality leftovers, should be packed away in an organized manner, only to be brought out again soon and dealt with. In this way, we have a sense of closure for each gathering without ever deluding ourselves into thinking that our work is done. Every time we gather people together in the name of Jesus, we need to depart from one another in such a way that it is clear we are people with a mission. The following story illustrates this. A priest was once taking some teens on a tour of the church. He asked them, "What is the most important thing in the church?" thinking that he would get responses about the altar, the tabernacle, or the crucifix. Instead, one teen responded, "The EXIT sign!" The priest, thinking the youth was being sarcastic, responded, "And why is that?" The youth said, "The EXIT sign is the most important thing in the church because it points us in the right direction for living out the gospel!" The youth had a clear idea of where the gospel truly takes place. It is true that the Mass certainly has closure. We are told, "The Mass is ended!" We sing a closing hymn. We process out. But closure is not finality! The close of Mass sends us on to the next thing: "Go in peace to love and serve the Lord and one another!" Anytime we gather people in Jesus' name, we must bring about a sense of closure by summarizing what has been accomplished, what needs to be accomplished, and how it will be accomplished. Finally, we need to send people forth with a sense of closure, fullness, or completeness that leads them to want to share their abundance with others. A healthy meal provides us with satisfaction, but even more important it provides us with the energy we need to go out and live our lives, to expend energy until the next meal!

Basket #11: Reflective Memories

The story of the Feeding of the 5000 is with us today because it was remembered. It became a part of the collective memory not only of the disciples but of the whole early Christian community who recalled it as a pivotal moment in their relationship with Jesus. Following the miracle event, people must have gathered around campfires, wells, and town squares for years to come retelling the story of the time Jesus found a way to feed 5000 hungry people with enough leftover to fill twelve baskets. As the story was told, no doubt people reflected upon what it meant to them. Today, we are a people with baskets full of memories left over from countless times that Jesus fed us and our ancestors. Without a basket to collect these stories, they risk being lost. When we recount how Jesus was present to us way back when, we become more aware of his presence in the here-and-now. As we bring gatherings of Jesus' followers to closure, we must never forget to preserve, gather, collect, and reflect upon the memories that have been established as we pass them on from gathering to gathering and generation to generation.

Basket #12: Faith in Jesus

We can have all kinds of baskets filled with all kinds of leftovers, but unless our gatherings result in an overabundance of faith in Jesus, we have accomplished nothing! The single most important leftover to be found in abundance, collected, and preserved is faith in Jesus as Lord and Savior. Without faith in Jesus, we run the risk of becoming civic organizations, humane societies, or political action groups. Nothing is wrong with any of the aforementioned, but faith in Jesus is what nourishes us, propels us, sustains us, and defines us. We are Christians . . . disciples of Jesus Christ, called to follow in his footsteps each and every day. The late, great Sr. Thea Bowman said it well once when called upon to be a keynote speaker at a diocesan evangelization conference called "Jesus Days" when she proclaimed: "*Every* day is Jesus Day!" When we gather in Jesus' name, set the table properly, and allow him to feed and nourish us, we will have satisfied an appetite that paradoxically becomes insatiable. Faith in Jesus leads to a desire to deepen faith in Jesus, a process that never ends. As we call people together in Jesus' name, let us never forget or allow them to forget that it is indeed in Jesus' name that we have gathered, and it is in Jesus' name that we are sent forth!

For Reflection

- Of these twelve baskets, which speak most strongly to your experience?
- Which of these twelve baskets is in greatest abundance in your place of ministry? Which are being neglected or could use more attention?

The Twelve Baskets Checklist

Number the twelve baskets in the following checklist in the order of importance as you see their need for the wellbeing of your ministry:

____ Ideas

____ Energy

____ Fellowship

____ New Disciples

____ Special Needs

____ The Establishment of Rituals

____ Evaluation

____ Charity

____ Unfinished Business

____ Closure

____ Reflective Memories

____ Faith in Jesus

Scripture for Prayer

Jesus said to them, "Amen, amen, I say to you, unless you eat the flesh of the Son of Man and drink his blood, you do not have life within you. Whoever eats my flesh and drinks my blood has eternal life, and I will raise him on the last day. For my flesh is true food, and my blood is true drink. Whoever eats my flesh and drinks my blood remains in me and I in him. Just as the living Father sent me and I have life because of the Father, so also the one who feeds on me will have life because of me. This is the bread that came down from heaven. Unlike your ancestors who ate and still died, whoever eats this bread will live forever."

—John 6:52-58

For I received from the Lord what I also handed on to you, that the Lord Jesus, on the night he was handed over, took bread, and after he had given thanks, broke it and said, "This is my body that is for you. Do this in remembrance of me." In the same way also the cup, after supper, saying, "This cup is the new covenant in my blood. Do this, as often as you drink it, in remembrance of me." For as often as you eat this bread and drink the cup, you proclaim the death of the Lord until he comes.

—1 Corinthians 11:23-26

In Their Own Words

Biologist Lewis Thomas has written that nature's great law for all living things is not the survival of the fittest but the principle of cooperation. Plants and animals survive not by defeating their neighbors in the competition for food and light but by learning to live with their neighbors in such a way that everyone prospers. God is the force that moves us to rise above selfishness and help our neighbors, even as He inspires them to transcend selfishness and help us. God pulls us upward out of ourselves, even as the sun makes the plants and trees grow taller. God summons us to be more than we started out to be.

—Harold Kushner

For Reflection

- How is the Lord calling you to be "more than you started out to be"? How can the principle of cooperation play a part in your ministry to others?
- What impact does it have on your ministry to know that the "bread" you serve brings everlasting life?

Suggested Activities

- Observe your attitudes and practices concerning leftovers at your meals. How can they be applied to the way you will approach "leftovers" in your ministry?
- Bring a basket with you whenever you minister as a reminder to gather up the leftovers from your gathering. Invite people to fill the basket with ideas, evaluations, comments, etc.

- Trace the roots of your present ministry. Where did the idea come from? Who was your predecessor? How is your ministry the result of "leftovers" from previous ministers or ministries?
- Take a camera or camcorder with you to your ministry and invite someone to capture the energy, ideas, activities, and rituals that have become a part of your gatherings. Post these photos or view the video occasionally as a reminder of the "leftovers" from your gatherings and the nourishment these memories can continue to provide.

Conclusion: ". . . *what was left of the fish*"

The story of the Feeding of the 5000 contains one of those little mysteries that the gospels seem to include from time to time. When the disciples collect the leftovers, the story tells us that "they picked up twelve wicker baskets full of fragments and what was left of the fish."

What I want to know is, how much fish was left over?

It seems strange that the author tells us exactly how many baskets of bread were collected but then leaves the amount of fish left over a mystery. This unresolved detail is like the story of the Prodigal Son when we are left wondering if the older son ever enters the party. Or, like the story of the rich young man who goes away sad, we wonder if he ever returns. We are once again left to our own imaginations to solve the mystery of the fish. It could be that the author just didn't see the fish as such an important part of the story. On the other hand, it could be that we are left to grapple with this small mystery because the author wants to remind us that ultimately we are not capable of gathering all of the Lord's abundance into our tiny little baskets.

The mystery of how much fish remained is a reminder to us, that what we are involved in *is* a mystery. We can come to some kind of an understanding of how Jesus feeds us and we can participate in some small way in the setting of the table for Jesus' meals, but in the end, we are dealing with a mystery of faith, namely, that Jesus is the Bread of Life. Unless we bring our hunger to Jesus, we risk spiritual starvation. In some mysterious way, Jesus takes what little we have and turns it into abundance. In some mysterious way, Jesus turns enormous crowds of 5000 into communities of faith. In some mysterious way, Jesus involves *us* in the setting of the table and the collecting of the leftovers. As we look out at the people gathered before us and see the enormity of their hunger and the apparent scarcity of our own resources, we can be confident that Jesus will respond to our "send them away" mentality with the words that have fed the multitudes throughout the ages: "*You* . . . give them something to eat!"

A Prayer for Using Leftovers

You feed us well, Lord, Bread of Life. You provide us with such abundance that we find enough left over to fill basket after basket. Thank you for blessing us with such abundance. Help us to never waste your gifts but to find ways to creatively preserve and share your goodness. Knowing that you provide for us, let us never fear the hungers of your people. Instead, tell us to give them something to eat, and we, in turn, will give them you!

Acknowledgments

The excerpt on pages 20-21 is from a September, 1966, speech by Dr. Martin Luther King Jr., as recorded on *In Search of Freedom* (New York: Polygram Records, 1995).

The excerpt on page 32 is from *It Takes a Village* by Hillary Rodham Clinton (New York: Touchstone, 1996), pp. 11-12.

The first excerpt on page 33 by Dag Hammarskjöld is quoted in *The Oxford Book of Prayer* edited by George Appleton (New York: Oxford University Press, 1985), p. 265.

The second excerpt on page 33 is from *A Simple Path* by Mother Teresa (New York: Ballantine Books, 1995), p. 73.

The difference between the "home run" mentality and "Wee Willie Keeler" mentality from page 41 is described in *A Passion for Excellence* by Tom Peters and Nancy Austin (New York: Warner Books, 1985), pp. 152-164.

The excerpt on pages 44-45 is from *Radical Grace* by Richard Rohr (Cincinnati, OH: St. Anthony Messenger Press, 1993), p. 254.

The first excerpt on page 45 by Roger Crawford is from *Playing From the Heart* and is quoted from *Chicken Soup for the Soul* by Roger Crawford (Deerfield Beach, FL: Health Communications, 1993), p. 252.

The second excerpt on page 45 is from *Awaken the Giant Within* by Anthony Robbins (New York: Fireside, 1991), p. 44.

The first excerpt on page 46 is from *More Than Meets the Eye* by Patrick Collins (Mahwah, NJ: Paulist Press, 1983), p. 23.

The second excerpt on page 46 is from *Stories of Faith* by John Shea (Chicago: Thomas More Press), p. 95.

Father Patrick Brennan's list of effectiveness skills for ministry on pages 58-59 is taken from *Re-Imagining the Parish* (New York: Crossroad, 1991), pp. 77-78.

The quotation on page 62 is from *Building Christian Communities* by Stephen B. Clark (Notre Dame, IN: Ave Maria Press, 1972), p. 20.

The excerpt on pages 68-69 is from *The Seven Habits of Highly Effective People* (New York: Fireside, 1990), pp. 192-193.

The excerpt on pages 86-87 is from *Here and Now* by Henri Nouwen (New York: Crossroad, 1994), pp. 82-23.

The excerpt on page 108 is from *When All You've Wanted Isn't Enough* by Harold Kushner (New York: Pocket Books, 1986), p. 183.

Joe Paprocki has provided several helpful insights to catechists and pastoral ministers alike over the past two decades. He is the author of *Tools for Teaching* and the video *Empowering the Catechist* (both from Twenty-Third Publications) as well as two mini-courses in the *Developing Faith* series for teens from Ave Maria Press, *Jesus, Should I Follow You?* and *In the Beginning*.

Currently a catechetical consultant for the Office for Religious Education in Chicago, Paprocki was a Pastoral Associate and Director of Religious Education at St. Mary of the Assumption parish on Chicago's south side from 1990 to 1997. He has a Master of Arts Degree in Pastoral Studies from Loyola University of Chicago.